I0461257

Cycle Breaker

A Guide to Transcending Childhood Trauma

Mindi Kessler, PhD

CYCLE BREAKER
A Guide to Transcending Childhood Trauma

Copyright @ 2022 Mindi Kessler, PhD
Published by Kessler Publishing; mindikessler.com.
Publication: September 6, 2022
All rights reserved. No part of this book except for brief quotations for review may be reproduced or transmitted in any form or by any means without written permission from the publisher.

Contact: support@mindikessler.com

mindi
KESSLER PhD

This book reflects the author's recollections of her own experiences over time, rendered to the best of her ability. The names and identifying details of all clients have been changed.

Editorial and production management:
Robyn M Fritz, Alchemy West

Design and layout:
Robert Lanphear, Lanphear Design

Cover design: Monica Wells

Copyeditor:
Laurel Robinson, Laurel Robinson Editorial Services

Library of Congress Control Number: 2022911893
ISBN: 979-8-9864933-0-5
Ebook ISBN: 979-8-9864933-1-2

Dedication

To Kyle, Grace, and Molly:
I am infinitely grateful that you are my family.

Contents

Foreword

When I was working toward my PhD in clinical psychology about fifty years ago there was a lively debate among professors and students about how "real" developmental trauma was and what its significance might be in understanding psychological problems and mental health diagnoses.

Some thought it was a fiction. Most thought that although it most likely was present, it was also much less prevalent than some might think and easily treatable using an assortment of cognitive-behavioral interventions. When I was asked to develop a program to treat the effects of child abuse early in my career, it became clear to me that trauma most certainly existed in those who had experienced child abuse and neglect. However, it took a number of years before I realized how pervasive its symptoms were and how difficult it was to help children and youth resolve their traumas. It was challenging to help them develop an integrated life that was not significantly impacted by having experienced verbal, emotional, physical, and sexual assaults in their homes, with their own parents being the perpetrators.

When I realized the eclectic therapeutic training that I had received did not adequately provide me with a means to offer effective therapy I developed my own model of comprehensive interventions (therapeutic, parenting, educational) for those who had been traumatized. This model of intervention became known as Dyadic Developmental Psychotherapy

(DDP) and it was influenced by my knowledge of attachment, intersubjectivity, trauma, and eventually neurobiology. I also developed a training program for other professionals who were struggling to provide a more effective intervention model for children who had experienced complex, developmental trauma.

When trauma occurs within your family and your attachment figures are unable to prevent it, especially when they cause it, its effects are likely to be persistent and pervasive. If you trust that your parents will keep you safe and your trust has been betrayed, it will be hard to trust them again. You are even likely to mistrust other adults, such as your teacher or therapist, who are caring and committed to what is best for you. To protect yourself from future relational trauma you are likely to not see or believe signs of safety from caring adults. In effect, those who hurt you in the past are still hurting you by making it very hard to trust others enough for you to heal.

The challenges these individuals face well into adulthood as well as the interventions that might help them begin to trust again are presented in this book by Mindi Kessler, PhD.

One of my early students, Dr. Kessler quickly demonstrated her clinical sensitivity and commitment to offering aid to traumatized children. Now when I read this powerful work, which follows her own personal path through pervasive relational trauma, I understand trauma more deeply than ever before. I am certain that if professionals had read it years ago they would not have minimized or questioned the impact of trauma on human development.

Dr. Kessler shares with us many moments in her life in which she experienced extreme pain at the hands of those she trusted—her parents. This caused her to create barriers to remembering and feeling this pain in order to survive, but at great expense to both her mind and body. With brutal honesty she presents the origins and consequences of her trauma and how she dealt with it. While at times it is painful to read Mindi's story, it helps us be more prepared to heal our own trauma, and, if we are practitioners, more able, through empathy and understanding, to help clients resolve their traumatic pain. That is her gift to us. She also offers a better understanding of specifically how the traumatized may become empowered to challenge and move beyond their trauma.

Yes, Dr. Kessler has become a cycle breaker for herself, and, through this book, for many others. In her personal experience and her professional practice she has found ways to help those who have also been betrayed in their early attachment relationships to overcome trauma.

Successful interventions require both our minds and our hearts. Dr. Kessler has awakened and fostered the development of both.

Daniel Hughes, PhD
Founder and Developer,
Dyadic Developmental Psychotherapy (DDP)

The Cycle Breaker Way

I am a cycle breaker. Maybe you are one, too. Or maybe you want to be one. We become cycle breakers by recognizing that we want more for our lives.

We are willing to do the courageous work of identifying the destructive patterns that our parents passed down to us. The ones their parents passed down to them. The same ones that we are trying to not pass down to our children or use to sabotage our relationships with others.

These patterns can include behaviors such as having problems setting boundaries; being excessively angry, controlling, or perfectionist; or being addicted to anything that helps us numb ourselves from pain.

The presence of destructive patterns in our lives is often an indicator that we have experienced developmental trauma. Developmental trauma occurs when children do not feel safe and/or are made to feel unworthy. When children are harmed, it shapes how they see themselves and the world. Their responses to trauma get wired into the brain, body, and psyche and penetrate every area of life, infiltrating their nervous system, character development, and ability to trust.

Developmental trauma can result from experiences of extreme abuse, including physical, mental, emotional, and sexual abuse. Developmental trauma can also occur with infractions such as routinely being told you are too much trouble, having overly strict parents who limit your choices and freedom, or feeling unimportant because your parents spend little time with you.

The need for cycle breaking emerges for adults who are unable to find peace in the present and no longer want to be controlled by the past. Cycle breakers are prepared to stop suppressing pain and are ready to create space for a bountiful future. This requires self-reflection and a willingness to address past wounds and move forward.

We cycle breakers take personal responsibility for our well-being by releasing apathy or blame and bitterness and becoming a deliberate creator of our lives. The process of healing restores our connection to Essence, the Divine part of us that never doubts or judges. Our Essence is always lovingly guiding us through every step on our path. As we allow ourselves to fully embrace and connect with this part of us, we become vibrant and alive.

People who are cycle breakers in the making know what they don't want but often lack the confidence and knowledge to put the past to rest and resuscitate a life that has been depleted of ease and joy. That was the case for me. I had an assortment of trauma symptoms that I had not identified as trauma symptoms. My body was permanently tense, and I suffered from chronic pain conditions, insomnia, autoimmune issues, and extreme fatigue. I was very hard on myself and mindlessly engaged in people pleasing, perfectionism, and workaholism. I was depressed and in awe of people who were not. I was stressed all the time.

For many years I tried to feel better, but I could not. I worked with a variety of professionals to find out what was wrong with me. At the time, our society was not very aware of how childhood trauma was reflected in the symptoms I had. I felt hopeless, unable to understand why I was so physically and emotionally miserable. When I thought I had exhausted all my options for feeling good, I had an awakening experience that showed me I had barely scratched the surface.

I agree with Maya Angelou, who said, "There is no greater agony than bearing an untold story inside you." Keeping secrets, such as not telling people about the abuse we experienced, takes an immeasurable toll us. I reached a point where I was no longer willing to further wound myself by suppressing the story inside me. This book reflects my cycle breaker journey. This is the story of how I transcended the pain from extreme childhood abuse and created a life I love. I now teach others to do the same.

It's important to consider the following questions if you want to create a life you love. Is what you are doing now working for you? Are you happy, or are you resentful? Do you have peace in your life, or do you feel out of balance? Are you living the life of your dreams, or are you observing others live theirs while you watch with a chip on your shoulder?

To live a meaningful life we must examine big questions like why we're here, why we have suffered, and what healing means. When we persistently seek the truth, we will find the answers. As you find your answers, you find your way back to yourself and reunite with your Essence, the Divine part of you that has been with you all along.

I offer this book as a guide as you aspire to be free from the confinement of trauma and an unfulfilled life. Every reader will be at a different place on their journey. Some concepts may immediately resonate. Others may be very triggering or may not feel true at all for you. It is important to digest and integrate what works for you and let the rest go. As we each progress on our journey, our consciousness expands, and we are more prepared to embrace principles about personal growth that once felt dismissive or confusing. If something doesn't "land" for you now, maybe it will later. As a teacher, coach, and therapist, it is not my job to tell people what to think or believe, but rather to help them find their own truth.

Although I have learned a great deal about suffering and healing, I still have a lot to learn. Thi   s book reflects what I feel to be true at this point in my human experience. I am thankful to the many healers, authors, and teachers I have learned from and the courageous clients who have sat on my couch, bravely sharing their journey with me. Some of their stories are included here with their permission. Their names and personal characteristics have been changed to respect their privacy.

Before you begin this book, I invite you to create a safe space for yourself. Consider the important elements to put in place that will allow you to feel comfortable and supported as you read and process this information. You may want to light a candle and grab your favorite cozy blanket, crystals, and essential oils before reading. Or you may want to read with a friend who is on the same path. You can also wear your favorite cardigan, the one that feels like a hug, or take a warm Epsom salts bath.

You may wonder if you could still benefit from this book if you don't think you have experienced developmental trauma. Everyone has faced difficulties, both in childhood and as an adult. You may simply be unaware of the toll these experiences have taken on you. This book is essentially for anyone who wants to live a fulfilling life. No matter the degree of hardship you have faced, this book is for you.

I am honored that you have chosen to read my book. You have what it takes to become a cycle breaker and create a beautiful life.

I'm rooting for you.

Preface

My childhood was very difficult. I was raised by parents who were quite wounded and uncaring. They married when my mom was seventeen and my dad was twenty-four. In just over two years, they had two children. I am the youngest.

As the oldest daughter in a family of seven children my mom had to care for her siblings, but it was clear that she did not know how to nurture. Maybe she did not receive warmth from her parents and so had none to pass on. Her mother was always kind to me, and I felt loved by her, but we didn't live close by, and so I had little contact with this one loving presence. We did not see my mother's father very often, but there was a darkness in him that persuaded me to avoid him.

My dad was one of two boys. His mother and his alcoholic father divorced when he was young; he was raised by a single mother and lived in poverty. I was told that he was regularly disappointed as he waited for visits with his father that didn't happen. He told me about being home alone with his brother, hiding under the kitchen table and holding a knife for fear of someone breaking in. I don't know everything they went through growing up, but I know enough to know my parents both dealt with substantial childhood trauma.

Completely overwhelmed with two young children and without their own sense of security, my parents repeated the abuse and neglect they experienced with my brother and me. They didn't seem to like each other or their children. They were remarkably angry, intolerant, and punitive. I came into the world as a traumatized baby, saturated in the womb with the fear and coldness that consumed my mother. It never got better.

Throughout my youth, I was immensely vulnerable. By age three I was an astute observer, an expert at body language. Maybe sooner. I fine-tuned my ability to predict, as much as anyone could, how the various tones in my parents' voices correlated with rage, condemnation, or the dreaded silent treatment. I studied facial expressions and body language to quickly detect shifts in their moods that could end in hostility and criticism. And then I braced myself, until bracing became my permanent state.

I was starved for love and warmth in a family that had very little to give. The neglect I experienced fueled a desperation for kindness, but it was dangerous to seek it from my empty parents. I often denied my impulse for connection to prevent rejection, which I believed was remarkably likely because of my parents' disdain for being burdened by my needs. I felt totally alone except for the kindness of my schoolteachers and some good friends, but no one knew how incredibly damaging my home life was.

My parents were easily angered and highly volatile. It was clear I could never do anything right in their eyes, which left me feeling frozen most of the time. My brother learned by their example that treating me with contempt was the norm, and I did not feel safe from him, either. Permanent hypervigilance was a requirement: I often contemplated how to choose the behavior that would most precisely limit the harm I endured. This made me strive for perfection, which was impossible: How could I precisely choose the right response, the right action or inaction, that would increase my odds of connection and decrease my odds of attack? It's no wonder I was so anxious, had headaches and stomachaches, and was always exhausted. Abandonment and terror are consuming.

The sexual abuse from my father started when I was quite young and continued for many years. I believe it started when I was so young that my body never had the chance to settle into the blueprint of a healthy body. This was the origin of the pelvic pain and resulting agony I felt for thirty years, which interfered with all parts of my life.

Despite the overwhelming evidence that my parents were guilty of brutality toward me, I protected *them*. I internalized their feelings of hatred for me, and I learned to hate myself. Incapable of managing a betrayal so vast, I suppressed my rage and turned it inward. Acknowledging my pain would have forced me to face the unbearable truth of being totally alone, which I could not do, so I developed ways to cope. I masterfully evolved skills of suppression (don't feel), denial (don't acknowledge the truth), and self-sacrifice (don't need anything). I buried my authentic self so deeply I no longer even knew who I was. My entire existence revolved around finding safety, and it was a complicated pursuit.

I constructed my day to limit being harmed. I was hyper-focused on avoiding and preventing the constant criticism, yelling, screaming, hitting, judgment, and just plain meanness in my home. This left no bandwidth for creativity, fun, self-expression, and freedom. I could not both enjoy myself and maximize my safety. Joy, happiness, and fun would take me off my game, and there was no room for error.

As a child, I did not know my parents were traumatized people who behaved without realizing what they were doing. I did not know their hatred for me reflected their own self-loathing. Instead, I thought there *must* be something wrong with me. I thought if I could be perfect, my parents would not hate me so much. It is unfortunate that I did not know the real cause of their abuse. If I had known, perhaps I could have been saved decades of feeling worthless, unlovable, and wishing for my life to end. Maybe it could have prevented the impossible drive for perfection, which only made me feel like a chronic failure and a phony.

My adaptive methods of managing a difficult childhood saved my life. The distorted perceptions I created to ensure my survival allowed me to eventually leave my parents' home alive, even though devastatingly wounded.

After high school, I attended college. I went into the world like a prisoner who had just been released. Colors were brighter, people seemed nicer, and there were more possibilities than I ever knew there could be. Much like a wrongfully convicted prisoner, however, I did not trust. I regularly expected that I would be exploited, criticized, or harmed, but I was powerfully armed with skills to protect myself. I was expertly gifted at suppressing my own needs and pleasing others.

As an adult, the denial that protected me in childhood made it impossible for me to see the truth about my wounded family. Well into my adult years a substantial portion of my energy continued to be directed toward receiving approval from my parents and my brother, although I was consistently shown that their acceptance was not possible. I was like an abused dog, longing for love that would never come.

I moved through life as if through quicksand. Everything took enormous effort. Ambition and success masked my feelings of inferiority. Plenty of people validated me professionally, but the acknowledgment of worthiness I craved the most persistently evaded me. Worse, I had no ability to validate myself.

Anticipating my parents' visits, I cleaned my home from

top to bottom despite working full-time, raising two children, and being increasing challenged by chronic pain and illness. I wanted to impress my parents and win their approval by demonstrating how competent I was. I still eagerly hoped for validation from them. Why? I had a husband who adored me, colleagues who respected me, and children who looked up to me. Why wasn't all of this enough to bring happiness? I shamed myself because I felt ungrateful.

After four decades, the toll from abuse and the lack of self-love made it nearly impossible for me to function. Exhaustion, illness, depression, hopelessness, and lack of worthiness finally superseded my ability to pretend I was okay. I crossed a threshold whereby I no longer could deny the devastating impact of how I grew up. My body, out of love for me, said "enough" as I nearly completely collapsed. Scared, but also relieved, I stopped fighting to keep up the façade.

My health crash forced me to set aside my professional endeavors, which allowed me to focus on healing. Determined to pull myself out of a very dark and deep hole, I tenaciously pursued wellness. Staying stuck was no longer an option. I committed to doing whatever it took to transform my pain into well-being. This dedication to myself brought tremendous learning and growth. The mystery of why I struggled with so much physical and emotional pain was solved as I released my well-rehearsed coping tools of denial and suppression and allowed myself to know the truth about the horrific abuse that had consumed my childhood.

Layer by layer, the trauma I experienced came to the surface. Over the course of many years, with the help of a variety of supportive and wise healing professionals, I addressed the pain stemming from the long-standing and extensive physical, mental, emotional, and sexual abuse, which had prevented me from experiencing the fulfillment in life I craved. The journey was massively difficult, and I was brought to my knees in anguish many times as I dealt with severe physical pain and emotional devastation, recognizing the depth of betrayal I had experienced.

As I healed, I became less of the insecure and wounded person I had been my whole life and became more aligned with my Essence. I learned how to have love, compassion, and acceptance for myself. I came to understand that the experiences in my life ultimately had a noble and Divine purpose. My mission in life has always been to assist others in recovering from deeply painful life experiences. This was decided before I was born. My childhood experiences gave me the information necessary to be prepared for this mission. My healing allowed me to align with my purpose.

Over time, I transcended the trauma from childhood, enabling me to develop a deep sense of joy, peace, and love. My life improved in every way as I healed.

The payoff of healing has been creating a life I love and stopping the intergenerational transmission of abuse in my family line. I became a *cycle breaker*.

Introduction

This book reflects a deep professional and personal exploration of trauma recovery and human capability. My approach for transforming trauma is based on what I have learned in my work as a therapist since 1997, studying and practicing many excellent trauma-resolution treatment approaches, including Eye Movement Desensitization and Reprocessing (EMDR), Somatic Experiencing, Logosynthesis, and Dyadic Developmental Psychotherapy.

My approach is also largely rooted in the wisdom I have gained in the process of transforming my own trauma. I have explored a wide range of mind, body, and spirit modalities in the teachings of many authors, teachers, and healers. I have learned from those who have guided me out of the darkness and from the clients I have assisted out of theirs. My quest to alleviate both my own suffering and that of those who have sought my help has informed my perspective about what it takes to transcend a painful life.

On the reality television show *The Voice*, gifted amateur musicians audition for the chance to be coached by one of the music industry's top stars. In one episode, coach Gwen Stefani said to a musician after his heartfelt performance, "Thank you for not wasting your pain." Even though she didn't know his story, it was clear that his performance was more compelling because of what he had been through. When we channel the wisdom gained from suffering into a higher purpose, healing is contagious.

I know I am far from alone in experiencing severe trauma. I wrote this book to share my truth and to offer a voice for the countless suffering adults who are plagued with feelings of worthlessness, powerlessness, and hopelessness, many of whom are unable to understand the origin of their own self-loathing and unhappiness. People who support wounded adults, such as partners, friends, and healing professionals, can also benefit from this book. It is for anyone who would like a road map to create a good life.

Cycle Breaker is part memoir and part guide to assist people recovering from developmental trauma, also known as complex post-traumatic stress disorder. Developmental trauma results from painful childhood experiences, ranging from being routinely dismissed and criticized to severe chronic abuse and neglect. Though developmental trauma begins in childhood, the profound impact is felt throughout life, until the wounds from childhood are healed. Using this book, traumatized people can get the information they need to better understand themselves and to find a pathway to healing.

Many people with developmental trauma live with a range of difficult symptoms and believe they are incapable of changing their lives. But I do not believe that you are stuck feeling the way you do. It is entirely possible to create high levels of joy and peace in your life, no matter what you have been through. Post-traumatic growth is the process of creating an even more vibrant and meaningful life after struggling with and transcending trauma. To achieve this, you must understand the necessary components of healing and dedicate yourself to doing what it takes to restore your sense of authenticity and return to your Essence, your true nature.

Essence is the part of us that is all knowing and all encompassing. It has no beginning and no ending; it is our eternal self and our contact with truth. This part of us is always growing and evolving and contains all the information we have gathered from all our lifetimes. Our Essence holds the qualities of joy, playfulness, and ease. It is awakened to the true nature of reality and is not hindered by personality, ego, and pain. Essence is hard to fully define because I do not believe we have the capacity to comprehend the magnitude of this Divine force that exists both within us and outside of us. Before our incarnation, Essence determines what it wants to learn more about during our human life and guides us to carry out this fluid plan. Though it is not a concept specific to the healing method called Logosynthesis, this powerful approach to transformation is my source of inspiration for using *Essence* as the word that represents the Divine in all of us.

Although we are born connected to our Essence, we are immediately exposed to programming from parents and society about how we are supposed to behave, think, and be. When we are wounded and not living an intentional life, we get more and more detached from our Essence as each year passes. Healing our trauma and breaking the cycle enables us to restore our connection to this vital part of ourselves.

Being a cycle breaker means you are the person in your ancestral line who puts an end to destructive intergenerational patterns. You are the courageous one who recognizes that how you were raised was harmful to you, and you don't want to repeat the same patterns in your life. In many cases, this is related to abuse and neglect. The destructive patterns can also be the result of over-functioning parents who did not teach you to believe in yourself; therefore, you may struggle with helplessness and the desire to be rescued. Choosing the cycle breaker way can allow you to recover from the hardships of childhood and live an empowered life, instead of repeating the transgressions made by previous generations. This requires you to face all you have been through and commit to loving yourself. It is no easy task, but it is worth it. Transcending childhood trauma is an inspirational endeavor, one you will never regret.

There are many possible points of view to explain why we experience hardship. The perspective we choose determines how we feel. Early in my journey of trauma recovery I heard a motivational speaker say, "Imagine what is happening in your life is happening *for* you, not *to* you." At the time this was a revolutionary idea because I believed I was powerless and victimized. I felt completely at the whim of life and unaware of my own power.

The speaker's message resonated deeply, serving as the beginning of my exodus from hopelessness. My perspective of hardship began to change as I reviewed my life through this lens. I could indeed see the many benefits that had accompanied the difficulties I faced. I could acknowledge that the trauma from my childhood enabled me to become a healer. I could see that though it hurt when people were taken out of my life, it was ultimately for the best. I felt more at peace with my health crisis, knowing it gave me the time I needed to rest and recover.

I became inspired to learn more, and I was drawn to other spiritual teachers who verified the notion that our highest good is always served by the experiences we face. As I began to understand more about the nature of suffering, I gradually started to believe that life was on my side and that hardship was not a punishment. My quest to understand suffering helped me to see that we are truly never alone, even if the support isn't in the form our human minds have been trained to expect. Paulo Coelho, author of *The Alchemist,* said, "And when you want something, all the universe conspires to help you achieve it." I began to believe that more was possible for me than I had previously realized.

I have come to understand that suffering is largely tied to expectations that certain things should or should not have happened and believing that life should or should not be a certain way. It is resistance to what was and what is. Even though people with childhood trauma expect hardship, we are conditioned by society to believe that challenges in life are unfair, and if we are suffering, it is the result of our own failure, the failure of others, or life having gone awry. When we think hardship is wrong, we respond with judgment and blame. We limit the possibility of empowerment, transcendence, and fulfillment when we believe that we were and are cheated or that we were or are alone.

Buddhist teachings describe the concept of the two arrows. The first arrow is the result of hardship. The sting of getting passed over for a promotion, dealing with a physical injury, or failing an important exam are experiences that can feel like we were assaulted. It hurts. According to this teaching, the second arrow is our reaction to the first arrow, when we add to our own suffering because of our judgment of what happened. We cannot control the first blow, but we can refuse to injure ourselves with our response. Knowing that hardship is part of a universal process can shift our perspective from victimhood to empowerment, from "Please, please, please don't let this be happening" to "I've got this."

There is an arc to the process of transformation. This means there is a predictable sequence of stages that one goes through when faced with adversity. Some refer to it as the hero's or heroine's journey. These are frameworks by which we can understand that hardship is a universal, and even beneficial, part of life.

Here is my own conceptualization of this process for cycle breakers.

Disconnection is where the journey is initiated. This is where the loss of innocence occurs. Wounding from parents or others happens, which alters our blueprint of ease and trust. The template of fear and unworthiness becomes the replacement. We learn to cope with pain instead of just being ourselves by following our own impulses, interests, and desires. The heart develops armor, and we operate to preserve our safety instead of living in integrity with ourselves, where we would speak our truth if we felt safe. In our attempt to avoid more pain, what could have been movement toward expansion becomes constriction.

Anesthesia is the period of life where we live in denial about our pain. We pretend we are okay. We rely on addictions such as mind-altering substances, being popular, being invisible, or any compulsive method to ward off the reality of how we really feel. We force the pain into hiding because we believe there is no solution to the suffering embedded in facing it. We do the best we can. For some this looks like overachieving by getting advanced degrees and important jobs to remedy the emptiness inside. For others, it can look like underachieving by living beneath our capability and being disconnected from life.

The *Crisis* is our wake-up call. This is the call to turn inward. This stage involves life as we know it coming to a halt as the result of life-changing circumstances. This may be a serious car accident, a chronic or life-threatening illness, a devastating divorce, or the loss of a job, home, or loved one. This is generally a very painful time, as the feelings of uncertainty that accompany the rug being pulled out from under us can be scary. How we appear to others suddenly becomes less important than finding a solution to the true cause of our suffering. The adversity makes it nearly impossible to continue living life as usual. We can ignore the wake-up call; it is a choice. However, for those who ignore or delay their response to the call, life only becomes more challenging and unsatisfying.

The *Revelation stage* is the part of the journey where we begin to realize why we are unhappy, and we mobilize our efforts to resolve our pain by dealing with the root cause. This is where our personal dragons appear and we learn to conquer them. We are tested with challenges we need to face to find our way back to our Essence. This is where we cultivate resiliency, internal strength, personal power, and self-love. In the Revelation phase we go beyond our own perceived limits and discover the power we have within ourselves. Just like Dorothy in *The Wizard of Oz*, we will find that we had it in us all along but could not access our capabilities until we were tested. Though this phase may feel isolating, we may also feel divinely guided. Many people have fascinating mystical experiences during this time, as the veil thins between the earthly and spiritual realms.

Finally, we enter the stage of **Completion**. This is the phase of the journey where we have transcended our pain and reengage with life as transformed people. We have reunited with our Essence and can now live with more joy and tranquility. We emerge like the phoenix rising from the ashes, the butterfly from the cocoon, the baby bird who has confidently left the nest. We learn to follow our intuition and align with our purpose. The jewels of wisdom that we discover on our quest are then shared with others to aid them on their transformational journey. There are still challenges in life, but now we have the confidence and wisdom to handle them.

There is tremendous value in cultivating wisdom; it is a requirement for a peaceful life. We cannot become wise through intellect; it must be embodied as the result of lived experience, which is the gift of a transformational journey. It is not just hardship that makes us wise: It is when we pair our experiences with knowledge and surrender that we allow ourselves to grow.

We are here on Earth to experience life. We must recognize that everyone experiences suffering and hardship. Though some people suffer more than others, no one gets a free pass. Once you have moved through your transformational journey, you will also know this to be true, not just with your mind, but with your whole being.

Pairing the helpful knowledge in this book with your experiences and willingness to let go can lead you to cultivate the wisdom that sets you free from suffering. This process enables you to become your own sage.

The transformational journey is an endeavor for all evolving people who are in the process of transcending childhood trauma. Everyone's journey is unique, but the process is the same: Disconnection, Anesthesia, Crisis, Revelation, and Completion. There can be great comfort in knowing you are not alone on your journey. Many people completed this journey before you; others are completing the journey alongside you or will begin theirs when yours is complete.

Although it may feel uncomfortable and triggering to see yourself in this book, I invite you to surrender your resistance and say yes to your healing journey. Resistance is bred from lack of trust and causes us to say no with our thoughts, words, and actions. Many of us were not allowed to say no in childhood. Many of us could not resist those who hurt us without suffering harsh punishment. Resistance is self-protection after a troubling childhood, but it can prevent us from moving forward. I invite you to say yes to the truth of what you experienced. I encourage you to say yes when you recognize how trauma impacts you. I welcome you to compassionately acknowledge your problematic patterns of thoughts, emotions, and behaviors stemming from unwanted childhood experiences. Say yes to lovingly embrace the journey that will bring you back to your Essence.

You can do it.

This book is divided into three parts.

"Part I: Origins" explains the roots of developmental trauma and how harmful parenting and other traumas create a foundation of fear and unworthiness.

"Part II: Consequences" addresses the complex challenges or consequences that wounded adults face as a result of growing up feeling unheard, unseen, and, for many, unloved.

"Part III: Empowerment" explores the 16 Pillars of Trauma Recovery, or the essential elements of healing that are necessary to transcend developmental trauma.

Let's begin.

Part I
ORIGINS

Uncovering the Origins
of Our Suffering

Our society tends to label, categorize, and judge people with little consideration for *why* they think, feel, and behave the way they do. We are all guilty of this. We do the same thing to ourselves. We assume we are deficient without considering the possibility that there is a good reason why we struggle. Judgment without curiosity creates fear, division, and isolation. When we can suspend judgment and instead seek to understand ourselves and one another, hearts open and healing occurs.

Behind every act of violence, from a school shooting to a brawl in a bar to an abused child or a sexual assault, is a perpetrator who is wounded and disconnected from his Essence. Separation from our Essence separates us from the humanity of others. When this happens, we become unconscious to the pain we inflict outwardly and inwardly. Disconnection from Essence is the primary cause of our suffering; therefore, removing all that blocks us from aligning with this part of us is necessary for trauma recovery.

How do we become disconnected from our true selves? For many, it starts almost immediately when we are born. Societal programming about how we are supposed to think, feel, and act often begins with the color of onesie we are placed in during our hospital stay as a newborn. This subtle and persistent conditioning continues as we watch our parents numb themselves with television, shopping, or alcohol after a hectic day of managing too many responsibilities because of the pressure to "succeed." We lose who we are when our parents say we are too much or not enough and when we are forced to suppress our emotions, words, and desires to be accepted.

Cultivating a fulfilling and fun life is a bigger task for those who had difficult beginnings. There is a steeper learning curve for navigating adult challenges when we are raised to fear our parents, our basic needs for love, affection, shelter, food, and safety are not met, and we are made to feel like we do not matter.

Part I explores why many people struggle to create a happy life after a difficult childhood. I explain how being raised by wounded parents sets up a foundation for people to encounter serious difficulties in life. I address what developmental trauma is, why caregivers hurt their children, and how attachment styles develop. I also examine how our belief system emerges, and how being unsafe in childhood makes us more vulnerable to further incidents of abuse. Finally, I describe the common ways children cope with overwhelming pain.

Chapter 1

What Is Wrong with Me?

Years ago I was lying next to my sleeping husband and contemplating how incredibly stuck I felt. I had a loving, encouraging, and devoted husband, but I did not appreciate him the way I felt I should. I did not know why. I had two daughters I adored, but I was not always heart-centered and patient with them. I had fulfilling work, but found myself functioning as a workaholic, which caused me to neglect myself and to be less present in my family. Unable to sleep that night, I asked myself the same questions I had considered a million times. *Why am I so unhappy? Why does my body keep failing me? Why can't anyone tell me what is wrong? Why am I not the mother or the wife I want to be? Why do I feel so alone? What is wrong with me?*

I scrolled through social media that night, something I don't recommend if you feel miserable. I was truly stumped. *What makes all these people seem so happy?* To be fair, it was highly possible that behind the smiling faces and declarations of being "blessed," people I envied were unhappy, too, but I could not even pretend anymore that life was good. I had suffered from physical and emotional challenges for as long as I could recall. I felt utterly at a loss to understand why nothing worked and why I was so incapable of feeling good. I was depleted and out of hope.

Eventually all my questions were answered. Understanding the reasons for my unfulfilled life involved an arduous process of uncovering dark truths about my traumatic upbringing. I had constructed a narrative about my life that allowed me to survive, but it prevented me from facing, processing, and healing what I had ignored: the abuse that pervaded my childhood. As this protective illusion dissolved, I experienced relief, devastation, and immense grief: I realized I would never be loved and accepted by the family that raised me.

When I finally realized my childhood experiences were at the heart of how dissatisfied and stuck I felt in life, I was not surprised. Even as an adult, I always felt more stressed and defeated after interactions with my parents. They did not treat me well, and I did not feel they truly cared about me. I had basically no relationship with my only sibling. He seemed to hate me most of my life, but I never understood why. Because I longed to have a close family, I still made numerous efforts to convince myself it was possible, despite our never being close or happy.

My healing process required me to dismantle the guise that had allowed me to appear to myself and to the outside world that I had it together. Like other kids with developmental trauma, I blocked out substantial and unbearable experiences to manage a life I could not change or escape. Maintaining contact with a family who never acknowledged the abuse and continued to devalue, judge, and dismiss me interfered with the freedom and safety necessary to heal. Though it took a long time, I made the difficult yet empowering decision to end contact with my family of origin.

As I uncovered the childhood trauma I experienced, my previously unexplainable symptoms made more sense. I better understood why I experienced suicidal ideation most of my life and why I persistently felt so critical of myself and others. I came to understand that the chronic pain I dealt with reflected decades of suppressed emotional pain and constantly bracing my body for danger. It was a relief to finally have an explanation for my suffering.

At this point in my journey, I have experienced extensive healing *and* I am still working to recover from my childhood. I have made sense of my life, though there is more to understand. I have learned to love myself, but sometimes I am self-critical and push myself too hard. I have largely been able to release resentment toward the people who hurt me, but at times I still feel angry with them. I regularly set healthy boundaries, though sometimes I don't. I have learned to regulate my emotional state, but sometimes I can't. I can easily cultivate feelings of joy and fun, but there are times when I feel low. I love and adore my husband, but sometimes we have misunderstandings, and there is still room for us to grow. I am a loving mother, but I can be distracted. Our family life is full of love, but sometimes there is tension. I am a happy person, and I am still evolving. We all have the capacity to grow until we take our last breath. That is my plan. In the words of Gwen Stefani, I am not wasting my pain.

Most of the clients I work with initiate therapy with no idea that traumatic experiences in childhood are the true cause of suffering. They present with concerns such as chronic stress, instability in relationships, and low self-esteem. I help clients uncover the origin of their challenges, which in my practice is always unhealed pain from childhood. Instead of encouraging my clients to ask themselves, *What is wrong with me?*, I steer them toward the more appropriate question: *What happened to me?*

Not only are children and adults often unaware of the impact of how they were raised because of survival coping mechanisms, but they may also not fully understand the toll of childhood trauma because of a concept called gaslighting.

Gaslighting is the process abusive adults use to convince the people over whom they have power that reality is not what it seems. It is a manipulation tactic used to paint the picture that everything is fine and the real problem is the victim's misperception. The abuser creates the illusion that the abuse did not actually happen. For example, the daughter who works up the courage to tell her mom her stepdad is sexually abusing her is told she must have misunderstood his actions. Parents gaslight neglected and deprived kids by shaming them for being selfish when they ask that their basic needs be met. The contradiction leaves children wondering if they experienced what they thought they did.

Gaslighting is a pervasive approach wounded parents use to silence family members. It creates enormous self-doubt in children who want to believe their parent is good. After being raised with this extremely confusing pattern, children have a distorted perception of what life was like. In essence, they were brainwashed to believe in a reality that never existed. They present with symptoms such as anxiety, depression, and addiction, and truly do not know why they feel the way they feel. Because of gaslighting in childhood, adults have difficulty fully acknowledging the truth of how they were raised. The absence of validation in childhood also teaches people to invalidate themselves.

People with a history of childhood trauma routinely minimize the hardships they have faced in life. In the beginning of therapy, they commonly make statements such as "I should be over this by now," "It was not that bad," and "Other people have it worse." They criticize themselves for being troubled by what they went through because they have learned to gaslight themselves. One client with significant challenges said to me,

"Please do not tell me this all has to do with mommy issues," as though it was a personal weakness that how she was treated in childhood affected her. It is important to understand how and why early childhood trauma has such a deep and persistent impact on us.

Many experts believe unprocessed trauma is a primary cause of chronic illness and many other mental health "disorders" such as anxiety and depression. The problem with a diagnosis is the prevailing societal belief that a pill will solve these tormenting conditions. In reality, these symptoms are signs that something much deeper needs to be addressed. Mental health symptoms are often normal reactions to painful life events. Merely treating symptoms will only delay attending to what needs to be healed to bring true relief to a person's suffering.

The journey of healing from childhood trauma takes tremendous courage. It requires us to be willing to acknowledge that our parents are not who we convinced ourselves they were, are, or could be. It requires us to make difficult decisions about setting boundaries with them and risking even further criticism, disapproval, and loss. However, the payoff for this work is enormous. Taking full responsibility for how we feel and addressing life from a place of personal strength instead of existing as a victim is more satisfying than just about anything. Embarking on this journey will lead you to the truth: There is nothing wrong with you.

Chapter 2

What Happened to Me?

Many, if not most, difficulties we deal with as adults have their roots in traumatic experiences that occurred when we were young, or even before we were born. Professionals are only starting to recognize the toll traumatic experiences take on us, especially those that occurred pre-conception, before birth, and to infants and young children. Many people believe that unless they experienced horrific criminal abuse, difficult childhood experiences should not be the reason for poor functioning as adults. However, unborn babies, infants, and children can experience troubling incidents, even some that appear minor, that lead to lifelong struggles. Some traumatic experiences are felt so deeply that the child's trajectory in life is changed forever. These types of traumatic experiences lead to what is called developmental trauma.

I define developmental trauma as "any occurrence or set of conditions before birth or early in life that fundamentally impacts children's sense of safety and security and/or their sense of worthiness." When traumatic experiences occur early in childhood, all aspects of the child's development are shaped within them. Children no longer look at the world as a safe place. Innocence is lost. Fear permeates every aspect of development, impacting both physiology and personality. When traumatic experiences in childhood are not resolved, they continue to significantly impact us into our adult lives.

Traumatic experiences influencing a child's development can result from in-utero trauma, from the intergenerational transmission of trauma through DNA from ancestors to descendants, from single incident shock traumas, and from varying degrees of chronic abuse and neglect. Though my primary focus concerns developmental trauma related to chronic abuse and neglect, I'll briefly explain other forms of trauma.

In-utero trauma can occur as the result of the mother's shock trauma or chronic stress from environmental factors. In some cases, the trauma for the unborn baby is experienced because of a chaotic environment that may include domestic violence, racism, sexual harassment, substance abuse, or the mother's inability to bond with her baby. Environmental stress can also occur when the mother is living in a war zone or is an immigrant or a refugee. When their mother is stressed, unborn babies feel it and produce their own stress hormones in response. A study measuring stress hormone levels in women who were pregnant during the 9/11 attacks showed that the children born to mothers with PTSD were more prone to becoming stressed after their birth than babies born to mothers who did not have PTSD (Brand, 2006). Exposure to stress in utero has been linked to low birth weight and preterm delivery (Bailey, 2010).

Intergenerational trauma, in which trauma gets passed down from one generation to another, can also lead to trauma symptoms. Many healers, such as Elizabeth Kipp, who is an Ancestral Clearing Practitioner, know that the unhealed trauma of our ancestors directly affects us. Science is starting to verify what has been called epigenetic inheritance, which means that the stressors of parents and ancestors "leave molecular scars adhering to our DNA" that causes behavioral and psychological alterations in their descendants (Hurley, 2015).

The descendants of Holocaust survivors have been a focus for investigations of intergenerational trauma. Researchers have found that Holocaust descendants can have changes in the structures of their brain, specifically the HPA axis, which is the primary system responsible for managing a person's stress response (Yehuda and Lehrner, 2018). A study at Emory University offered compelling evidence supporting the validity of inherited trauma. Researchers found that pairing the smell of cherry blossom with an electrical shock for mice created a conditioned fear response to the cherry blossom fragrance; when the mice were later presented with the cherry blossom smell without the shock, they still had a trauma response. Even more noteworthy, the offspring of these mice also exhibited a fear response when introduced to the cherry blossom smell, even though they had never been given an electric shock (Dias and Ressler, 2013).

Babies and children can also experience shock traumas because of their own direct experience of acute, single incident traumatic events. Examples of shock traumas include:

- Being in a car accident
- Falling from a changing table or other tall structure
- Witnessing an assault
- Getting bitten by a dog or other animal
- Painful medical procedures
- Life-threatening experience during labor and delivery

Although new parents can recognize that a problematic birth is a stressful experience, it is not commonly known that birth trauma can also be both emotionally threatening for the infant and the root cause of many emotional difficulties later in life. For example, an infant injured during the delivery process has started life in a state of threat and therefore may be imprinted with a profound sense that they are not safe, and thus can be very anxious. Children traumatized as babies have no conscious memory of this threat to safety, which makes it difficult for them and their parents to understand when seemingly irrational emotional and behavioral challenges emerge and persist.

In some cases, single incident shock traumas can resolve in the context of a loving relationship with a parent who can provide compassion, comfort, and intervention. Other times, single episode shock traumas can have a troubling and lasting impact. This can happen when children do not feel supported, or when parents are unaware an experience was traumatic and do not get their children the help they need.

Single incident shock traumas can have a big impact on a developing child, but in most cases children suffer more intensely from trauma as the result of ongoing abuse and neglect by their caregivers. The following are examples of childhood experiences related to abuse, neglect, or abandonment that are commonly associated with developmental trauma:

- Being raised by a parent with developmental trauma
- Being placed in foster care
- Being adopted at birth or later in childhood
- Losing a parent while young
- Being raised by a parent with chronic illness
- Parental depression during formative years
- Parental suicide
- Experiences of racism and other forms of targeted oppression

- Substance abuse in the family
- Domestic violence in the family
- Physical, emotional, mental, and/or sexual abuse
- Being bullied
- Being left unattended in a crib for long periods of time
- Being chronically criticized, judged and devalued by parents
- Being heavily controlled and given little freedom
- Being parentified and treated like an adult

Children who experience developmental trauma often feel incredible emotional pain. They grow up feeling powerless, helpless, hopeless, confused, and sad. They are often described as children with "oppositional defiant disorder" and "conduct disorder." Kids with developmental trauma can engage in behavior such as aggression, cutting, running away, sexual promiscuity, suicide attempts, and addiction. They are the children and teens society deem problematic, when, in essence, they are consumed with pain from abandonment by their parents and by a society that truly does not see, hear, or understand them.

Not all children with developmental trauma express their pain outwardly. Many internalize their symptoms and may look quite normal to the untrained observer. They can experience extreme anxiety and depression but may be surprisingly successful in some areas of their lives. They may become super-achievers who excel in school and extracurricular activities. Adults may admire their accomplishments but be unaware of the incredible pain driving their overwhelming need for success and external approval.

Life is not easy for adults who grew up with childhood trauma. Their unhealed pain can be reflected in long-standing patterns of anger and resentment, self-rejection, self-doubt, anxiety, depression, irritability, shame, guilt, sexual dissatisfaction, and general unhappiness. Most adults with developmental trauma have challenges in relationships. Additionally, there is a link between childhood trauma and chronic health problems. Making matters worse, not only do traumatized people face complex and multifaceted challenges with life, but often they do not know why life has been hard and why they feel unhappy.

When a person's expression of thoughts, emotions, and behaviors falls outside what is considered acceptable, society can be judgmental. It is important for all of us to understand that challenges dealing with life reflect a person's best attempt to manage a history of unmanageable experiences. Suffering can be reduced if, as a society, we can be more compassionate, understanding, and aware of the needs of traumatized children, and later of the adults they grow into. How do you mistakenly judge yourself or others for what you deem to be unacceptable when perhaps the behavior is merely an attempt to manage unbearable pain?

Chapter 3

Why Parents Hurt Us

It is easy when we are wounded to condemn the people who have harmed us. Our pain from abuse and neglect may convince us that the only way we can feel better is if those who have hurt us are held accountable. We may want a reckoning, where the truth is revealed and punishment is assigned. I personally understand this because this longing consumed me for many years.

The secrecy involved in abuse can feel like a prison, and it's natural to want the truth to prevail. However, vindication will not resolve our suffering. Neither justice nor revenge will heal us. It's highly unlikely that parents who seriously wound their children will take responsibility, and the longing for it impedes recovery. In the aftermath of developmental trauma we have a choice to make: Do we want to have a good life, or do we want to cling to the hope that our parents will acknowledge their failings? We cannot have both.

Anger at our parents is not wrong: It is normal for those who have suffered trauma to be angry. It is part of the process of healing to feel angry and even rageful toward those who forced their will upon us, ignored us, or both. Anger is an acknowledgment that we have been harmed, and it can provide the fuel we need to tend to our pain. Addressing anger and other emotions stemming from abuse and neglect is a complex step that cannot be skipped in trauma recovery. Gaining an understanding of why we have been harmed can enable us to more readily let go of our anger and our need for others to accept responsibility.

Therefore, one of the most important questions we can consider is "Why *did* my parents hurt me?" I have my own beliefs about this, but you are not required to believe what I do. In fact, to become empowered we must learn to think for ourselves.

I am not sure it's possible while we are here on Earth to fully understand why we were hurt by our parents or others. Our human mind cannot grasp the complexity of all the factors at play that contribute to deeply painful experiences. I'm also not sure we are meant to be privy to the entire explanation. However, I do believe we are capable of coming to terms with what happened in a way that can free us from the confinement of feeling victimized.

So why do parents hurt their children? From my point of view, there are a variety of reasons.

Many people teach that our soul is heavily involved in planning various components of our life before we are born. Caroline Myss explains how souls make agreements with one another, called soul contracts, to support each other's growth. In many cases the agreement reflects the adversity one soul will present to another, in human form. The disharmony related to the adversity creates the possibility of expanding our consciousness and achieving the goals we set forth for our human experience. Our soul wants to have a variety of experiences on Earth; this is how we learn. We cannot learn about betrayal by reading about it: We must experience it. From this perspective, we are harmed by our parents because we made a pre-life agreement to experience wounding from them, for the purpose of our soul growth.

Some people resist this point of view because they think it lets the people who hurt them off the hook. However, having agreements with our parents and others for how they will treat us in this life doesn't absolve them of responsibility. Even though my parents have not been held accountable for how they harmed me, they are not off the hook. They may not be mindfully aware of the guilt and shame they carry, but some part of them is suffering because of how they have treated me. Why? Because we cannot hurt another human without also wounding ourselves.

There is also the issue of karma, which essentially means cause and effect. We will need to feel both the harm and the good we cause to others, either in this lifetime or another, for the purpose of our own learning and growth. Those who hurt us in this life will experience what they have done to us. This can also be a reason that we are experiencing hardship, because of how we have previously harmed others. Karma is the means by which people are held accountable.

We also experience in life what Divine Intelligence determines is necessary. The Divine is a constant participant in our lives, bringing experiences to us and removing experiences from us. Some of these experiences may make sense to us, and some may not.

The concept of free will is also in the mix. Our personal will is an invaluable determinant of what we are able to accomplish and experience in life. What makes the human journey unique is our ability to learn, grow, make decisions, and impact our own life, as well as the lives of others. To a certain degree we are the creators of our life experiences because of our intention, focus, choices, and will. Others also have their free will, and their choices can enhance or interfere with ours. I don't know the degree to which free will can supersede pre-life planning and karma when it comes to the harm we face as children, but I do believe that Divine Intelligence always has the final say. It is up to each of us to sort out our beliefs about why we face adversity in life, including being hurt by our parents, in a way that allows us to find acceptance and peace. This includes both spiritual and human explanations.

On a human level, parents hurt their children because they are ruled by their unhealed pain. They operate from patterns they experienced in childhood, which are typically the same patterns that dictated their parents' behavior, such as fear of rejection, helplessness, and powerlessness. Though each wounded parent has an individualized story shaping how they relate to their child, what wounded parents have in common is the limited or complete inability to be compassionate toward them. This is often reflected in their absence of validation and empathy and in their failure to apologize for their mistakes.

The other commonality of many abusive parents is they do not consciously recognize that they have hurt their children. Because of their own complex system of navigating unhealed trauma, they can be incapable of recognizing the impact of their actions—and inactions. Unhealed pain leads to a need to self-protect and control others. Parents with these behaviors have been unable to break the cycle.

Most of my life I believed my mom intentionally hurt me. Her chronic criticism and punitive nature felt very personal. As a child, I truly believed she despised me. I have only one memory of her expressing compassion toward me. My dog killed my hamster when I was in elementary school. My mom did not really comfort me, but I saw tears in her eyes, which is the most warmth I ever recall experiencing from her.

I now believe she was so traumatized herself that she did not realize the magnitude of her cruelty toward me in childhood. I imagine she was consumed with the pain of her own childhood, which made being in a troubled marriage and raising children terrifying and overwhelming. She could not cope well. Her hurtful behavior was very likely her best attempt to protect herself and manage her unbearable internal life. I now believe she wanted to be a good mother, but just did not have the internal or external resources to become one.

The harm caused by my dad was more confusing. Sometimes he would be kind. Other times he was shockingly hurtful. Complicating matters was that my dad found it much easier to be his best self around people outside of our family. Away from the stressors of being in the difficult roles of husband and father, my dad was able to be likable, kind, generous, and warm toward others.

It was confusing to see how our community responded to my dad: They all liked him. I routinely heard, "I just love your dad." I developed enormous self-doubt as I juggled my own truth: *My father is mentally, physically, emotionally, and sexually abusive, and everyone else thinks he is wonderful. How can these two vastly contradictory behaviors exist in the same person?*

It's possible that my dad created the image of himself as a "good guy" so that no one would believe he was capable of abuse. It's also possible that he was simply less stressed around other people and was able to reveal a different side of himself. Maybe being a people pleaser with others invited the acceptance and validation he craved because he did not receive it as a child. I suspect my dad's manner of presenting himself to others as a likable guy allowed him to suppress the shame he may have otherwise felt about how he treated his family. It seems to me that my dad believed that his public persona was who he was. Image was his form of self-protection.

Many parents who hurt their children think they are being good parents. They may believe that control is love. They may justify their controlling behavior as necessary to protect their children from being spoiled or being harmed by others. They may also think overly strict parenting is necessary to help their children develop a thick skin so they will be less wounded by life.

I was stunned when I heard my dad tell someone he felt he and my mom had been good parents, but from his perspective he likely believed he excelled where his parents had failed. Maybe he felt that since he and my mom didn't divorce until I was an adult, they did a good job by providing a two-parent household. Perhaps he felt he was a good dad since we did not live with poverty the way he did. He coached our childhood ball teams, and he and my mom always attended our athletic and other school events. Maybe he viewed these behaviors as the hallmarks of good parenting.

Ultimately, my dad had a narrative that fit how he wanted to perceive himself, and it did not include the fact that his behavior was remarkably harmful to the people inside our household. It is still painful for me that his perspective about our family life is vastly different from mine. However, my journey of healing has invited me to see that the wounded boy inside my father would never have wanted to hurt his own children, and this softens my anger.

Addressing the hurt associated with abuse is necessary. However, no matter how much we want to make our parents wrong for their hurtful behavior, at some point it is simply not useful. Though I have worked with some parents who have been able to face and address how they have wounded their children, this is not the norm. The parents of most people with developmental trauma will never acknowledge that they hurt them. Those of us who aspire to be cycle breakers must make peace with this. Those of us who are advanced cycle breakers, who desire even deeper growth, accept our role as the healer of our lineage and willingly engage in both personal and ancestral healing, which benefits those who came before us and those who follow.

I have found in my many years of clinical practice that when people gain understanding about the psychological state of their caregivers, it can bring relief. Some parents who hurt their children have qualities of what the mental health community calls a "personality disorder." I am not a fan of psychiatric diagnoses: It can be harmful to pathologize people by labeling them as disordered. Most "disorders" are simply various manifestations of a trauma response.

Anyone with the symptoms associated with a personality "disorder" was a wounded child and is now a wounded adult. The symptoms associated with their challenging personality reflect their best attempt to cope with a traumatic upbringing. I address this topic to help adults who were raised by parents with difficult personality styles gain a deeper understanding about their parents, with compassion for both the troubled parents and the wounded children they have raised.

At times all of us can demonstrate attributes of difficult personality styles. None of us are innocent of overreacting, being absent, imposing our will on others, or feeling insecure. You may see attributes of your parents, or yourself, in the descriptions below. Don't make it wrong; just seek to understand.

Borderline Personality

"Walking on eggshells" is a phrase that describes what it is like to live with someone who has a borderline personality style. Anyone who knows someone with this presentation of trauma can relate to the uneasy and fearful feelings that emerge from being around someone who is often volatile. Children living with a parent who has a borderline personality are frequently on edge, anticipating threatening behavior.

When I suspect a client was raised by a parent with a borderline personality, I routinely share with them Christine Ann Lawson's book, *Understanding the Borderline Mother*. It offers a succinct chart comparing ideal parenting behavior with that of a parent with a borderline personality. It identifies the following behaviors as characteristic of borderline parents:

- Confuse their children
- Do not apologize or remember inappropriate behavior
- Expect to be taken care of
- Punish or discourage independence
- Envy, ignore, or demean their children's accomplishments
- Destroy, denigrate, or undermine children's self-esteem
- Expect children to respond to their needs
- Frighten their children
- Discipline inconsistently or punitively
- Feel left out, jealous, or resentful if children are loved by someone else
- Use threats of abandonment (or actual abandonment) to punish their children
- Do not believe in their children's basic goodness
- Do not trust their children

Parents with borderline personality characteristics have behavior that is often unpredictable, and can be rage-filled, critical, and dismissive or excessively passive. Children raised by these parents grow up without validation and often feel responsible for their parents' abusive behavior. The need to walk on eggshells around parents like this is a major reason we develop a compulsion for perfectionism and people pleasing.

Narcissistic Personality

People with a narcissistic personality have an enormous need for admiration and self-indulgence. They seek attention for beauty, power, status, and winning. Narcissists persist to get their own needs met, regardless of the cost to others, and with little to no awareness of how their behavior impacts people. They are often arrogant and entitled, evoking fear in others who do not succumb to their demands. Someone with this personality style is often described as "thin-skinned" and easily offended and is often hostile toward anyone demonstrating disloyalty.

Children raised by narcissistic parents must learn to abandon who they are because they are forced to yield to the demands of a parent who will never see or respect them. Elan Golomb's book *Trapped in the Mirror* precisely captures the experience of the child who is raised by a narcissistic parent: "A child wants to please his parents. If they are narcissistic and tell him how to feel, he stops knowing his own feelings. A narcissistic parent declares his child's natural feelings are wrong if they are in disagreement with his own" (p. 145). The children of a narcissist grow up in a constant state of fear; they experience criticism, control, and manipulation as a way of life and learn that objection is not a safe option.

Dependent Personality

Common behaviors for parents with a dependent personality style include an excessive need to be cared for by others, serious difficulty making decisions, and helplessness when left to handle basic responsibilities and child-rearing. Someone with a dependent personality is often afraid to be alone and will openly submit to the control of others to prevent abandonment. These caregivers are desperate for relationships, and when one ends, they often quickly start another. Their desperation can cause poor decisions about the adults they bring into their children's lives.

Children raised by dependent parents learn at a young age that they cannot count on them. Children in these families are treated as a confidant and peer and are often expected to take care of siblings and do excessive household work. This is known as *parentification*. Parents who act in a helpless manner create fear in their children, who are forced to sacrifice their childhoods. As one client told me, "I had to parent my parent."

In general, parents with the above personality styles lack the ability to self-reflect and self-regulate. Some parents with these traits are highly dissociated and largely, if not entirely, incapable of recognizing the impact they have on their children and others. Without a sense of security and self-worth, they find it impossible to parent in a way that fosters resilience and confidence in the children they raise. They are too wounded and disconnected from their own Essence. Unable to see their children as separate from them, their hurtful behavior reflects how they truly feel about themselves.

Many people ask me, "Did my parents really do the best they could?" Although it can be very challenging for us to accept the limitations of our parents, we imprison ourselves if we hang on to resentment. The journey of a cycle breaker is to find a way to stop blaming our parents for how they have hurt us without invalidating ourselves for the pain we experienced from their impaired parenting. To transcend childhood trauma we must let go of the viewpoint that our parents could have or should have done a better job parenting us. We can move forward in life only if we are willing to adopt a more productive viewpoint of the hardship we experienced growing up, which then enables us to commune with life more peacefully. I do not suggest this is easy: It can take a substantial amount of time and effort to accomplish this task of healing.

One way we can loosen our grip on the anger we feel toward our parents is to reflect on the times we have also hurt people, including being unkind, judgmental, and demeaning. This can help us understand and accept that when we are wounded, we can unintentionally and unknowingly hurt people. As Maya Angelou said, "I did then what I knew how to do. Now that I know better, I do better."

Our parents only did what they knew how to do and what they had agreed to do based on our pre-life agreement. I concluded that though I didn't like that I experienced abuse from my parents, it happened, I can't change it, and it was a necessary part of my human experience. I could be wrong, but this is the perspective that makes me feel more empowered.

My relationship with my parents would have been very different if they had felt safe and loved growing up. At some point, I realized it wasn't helpful to blame anyone at all, because the blame for my abuse did not lie solely with my parents. Yes, they were responsible, but trauma is complicated. They both had an extensive trauma history, as did the generations who came before them.

The trauma my parents experienced did not start with them. It also did not start with their parents. I now know that even though they hurt me, my parents were the right parents for me. I no longer identify myself as a victim (most of the time). I know that all I endured gave me the strength necessary to live the life my soul planned for me. It's been a remarkably hard journey, and it has given me the opportunity to heal lifetimes of trauma and pain and to develop the wisdom necessary to now experience life as an adventure instead of the burden I once felt it was.

I invite you to reflect on the behaviors of your parents or the adults who raised you. Do they fall into any of the categories of personality styles described in this chapter? If so, how did it feel to see your parent represented in this way? Did it validate, anger, or confuse you? Maybe you saw yourself in the personality-style descriptions, which could have felt destabilizing. If so, please be gentle with yourself. We can't help but absorb some of the mental, emotional, and behavioral patterns of the people who raised us. We often use the same coping methods our parents used because they are our childhood role models for navigating life.

The process of coming to terms with the limitations of our parents is something that takes time. We can't flip the switch from resentment to acceptance overnight. And even when we do gain insight about why our parents hurt us, there remains the journey of releasing our trauma and pain so we can authentically make peace with the fact that our parents were limited because of their own pain. Additionally, recovery from childhood trauma requires a determination to transcend the belief that we are still victims. Returning to wholeness relies on accepting what was and what is.

Chapter 4

Attachment

Attachment is a biological drive, the purpose of which is to elicit the care needed to feel safe. We are designed for secure attachment. Babies naturally use crying, grunting, smiling, laughing, and cooing to cultivate and fortify a safe and loving connection with parents.

When parents consistently respond with attunement, they are intimately aware of what is going on in the inner life of their child and respond in a manner that matches what the child needs. This shows children they can depend on them, and as a result, they feel secure and can develop trust in themselves, in others, and in life. A *secure* attachment enables us to stay more closely connected to our Essence.

With an *insecure* attachment style we lose connection to our Essence, which is our healthy navigation system. An *insecure* attachment style develops when parents are mis-attuned because of distraction, parent-child temperament mismatch, or neglectful or aggressive parenting. Medically traumatic experiences can also lead to insecurity. When we lack safety, whatever the cause, we lose the ability to trust.

Lack of a secure attachment to parents is a primary cause of developmental trauma. When we do not feel safe as children, we develop attachment patterns that center on avoidance, ambivalence, or disorganization, when no organized strategy is possible. Our attachment style falls on a continuum in which we have a predominant style of attachment but can also have characteristics of other styles. Identifying our attachment style can help us understand what triggers us in relationships and why we think, feel, and behave the way we do.

Avoidant Attachment

When children are raised by parents who consistently do not meet their needs, they develop an *avoidant* attachment style. Although these children are desperate for love, acceptance, and connection, they conclude that their parents are incapable of meeting their needs, so they give up on them to avoid the heartache of persistent rejection.

Children with avoidant attachment demonstrate excessive independence. They realize survival demands that they take on parental responsibilities, such as making their own meals and taking care of siblings.

Avoidant youth can become very stoic, as they have been conditioned to suppress emotion because their parents cannot tolerate it. Some parents cannot handle anger and frustration, and others are even intolerant of happiness and joy. To cope with their parents' low threshold for emotion, avoidant youth learn to swallow how they feel. They may use self-harming behavior to suppress the overwhelming pain of loneliness and despair that comes from feeling like no one cares.

Avoidant children grow into dismissive adults who remain self-reliant. They do not like to ask for help and often neglect their needs if it means depending on others. People with avoidant attachment can have low self-awareness because they typically deny or minimize the hurt that they felt growing up. As partners, these adults can feel threatened by intimacy. Vulnerability requires trust, which is very slow to develop for people with dismissive attachment.

One of my clients with an avoidant attachment style was distraught after the death of her beloved dog, Buddy. For a decade, this pet was her soul mate and her primary source of love and companionship. Growing up with a narcissistic father and dismissive mother, Zoe learned that getting her emotional needs met in a relationship with a human was unlikely, so she limited her vulnerability with people. Her dog offered the unconditional love she had always craved. The gift of Buddy's death was the motivation Zoe's grief gave her to begin the work of healing from her difficult childhood. She told me, "He saved me when he was here, and he saved me when he left."

Ambivalent Attachment

Inconsistent caregivers create ambivalence in their children. These parents are sometimes available, nurturing, and present and at other times they are absent, dismissive, or harsh. The possibility of even a little attention, affection, or approval motivates children to continue to seek attention from unpredictable parents.

Children with *ambivalent* attachment are anxious children. The lack of dependability from parents creates hypervigilance, where children are always prepared for the possibility of a threatening interaction. They can be people pleasers, disruptive kids, or both. They please to avoid rejection and to solicit kindness, or they "misbehave" because of overactive survival responses, demonstrated by a strong need for control. School creates many opportunities for fearful children to perceive the behavior of others as threatening. These children can be overly clingy with teachers, may argue or talk out of turn, or may be perfectionistic and high achieving. All these behaviors are driven by their need to be seen, heard, and feel they matter. Ambivalent children become preoccupied adults who can have challenging relationships with friends, coworkers, and partners. The insecurities initiated in childhood continue to feed a fear of abandonment and rejection, which can lead to off-putting behaviors. For example, people who try to impress friends and coworkers by talking extensively about their accomplishments and abilities may intend to impress others but actually annoy them by their self-centeredness.

I previously have primarily identified with an ambivalent attachment style. For much of my adult life I felt like a social misfit because others didn't accept me. I felt insecure, misunderstood, fearful of not pleasing others, and critical of myself.

I have also had elements of avoidant attachment style. I have had to work hard to allow myself to receive my husband's freely given love. After our first daughter was born, he gave me the gift of a journal he wrote during my pregnancy. At the time, I could not tolerate the love embedded in this gift. I thanked him and put it away, barely looking at it.

Healing my trauma has more closely aligned me with secure attachment. I feel much more relaxed with life and capable of handling adversity. I am thankful to now feel safe and at ease in my relationships. I can happily and easily receive my husband's love and affection, and I now truly appreciate the journal he gave me. However, there is always more room for us to develop a deeper sense of security with life. I still have more work to do.

Disorganized Attachment

Children develop a *disorganized* attachment style when no organized strategy works to cultivate some level of safety. These children are frightened of their parents' highly unpredictable, threatening, and often violent behavior. It is natural for children to seek a parent's comfort when they feel scared, but it is enormously confusing when they are also terrified of them. These children endure massive confusion, because both their attachment and survival systems are simultaneously activated. Confusion about how to handle a total lack of safety causes internal disorganization. This leads to frequent freeze states, where both the brake (parasympathetic nervous system) and the gas (sympathetic nervous system) are on, causing nervous system activation that can lead to unusual behavior.

One child I knew with disorganized attachment longed to feel a sense of belonging with his peers at school but was also terrified of them. Instead of walking up to the kids on the playground, he approached them in a crabwalk, which he believed would allow him to retreat more easily if threatened.

Adults with a disorganized attachment style demonstrate contradictory behaviors. Despite a desperateness for connection, they frequently push people away and may then blame others for abandoning them. These adults can repeatedly find themselves in abusive relationships because they can lack the capacity to recognize danger. Some adults with a disorganized attachment style may lack empathy and can dangerously exploit and harm others. They often have extreme fear of rejection, abandonment, and victimization.

Characteristics of Attachment Styles

Here are the characteristics of the different attachment styles.

Secure Attachment
- Demonstrates flexibility
- Able to compromise in relationships

- Full of confidence
- Able to easily repair problems in relationships
- Responds with resiliency to challenges in life
- Can easily assert self
- Can easily self-reflect
- Calming to self and others
- Easily feels gratitude and appreciation
- Can set good boundaries
- Values fairness

Avoidant Attachment Style in Adults, Also Known as Dismissive

- Excessive self-reliance
- Minimizes needs
- Limits emotional expression
- Uncomfortable with vulnerability
- May want to limit physical contact with others
- Can feel resistant or conflicted when others want closeness
- Denies or is unaware of childhood abuse
- Rigid, hyper-controlled
- Few or no memories from childhood
- Suppresses complaints or dissatisfaction in relationships
- May claim relationships are positive, contrary to evidence
- Communication can be overly succinct

Ambivalent Attachment Style in Adults, Also Known as Preoccupied

- Excessive dependence on others
- Excessive emotional expression
- Easily overwhelmed

- Can lack structure and boundaries
- Preoccupied with past hurts
- Communication can be excessive
- Can be sensitive to the possibility of rejection and abandonment
- Has a tendency to be blaming in relationships
- Can be difficult to please
- May be critical and abrasive
- Can be preoccupied with what is going wrong

Disorganized Attachment Style in Adults, Also Known as Unresolved

- Frequent dissociation
- Poor affect regulation: difficulty managing emotions, easily upset
- Can be impulsive
- Can be aggressive toward self and others
- May be abused in adult relationships

Our attachment style develops from a need to adapt to our environment. For some kids, it is adaptive to become avoidant. Self-reliance is a good survival strategy when parents are incapable of meeting their needs. Ambivalence is smart if parents are only sometimes available. Ambivalence keeps a child open to the possibility of receiving when the parent *can* give love.

Adults with an anxious attachment style have an outdated template for relationships. Being fearful of relationships during an unsafe childhood was protective, but fear in adulthood only reinforces dysfunctional patterns. Being cautious is good but being scared is a trauma pattern. Creating a secure attachment style involves healing our original wounds and the limiting beliefs that keep us insecure.

Dr. Harville Hendrix and Dr. Helen Hunt have a wonderful model for helping couples with insecure attachment strengthen their relationship. Authors of *Getting the Love You Want*, they describe imago theory, which illustrates how and why we select our mate. These authors explain that our subconscious mind, the part of us that diligently holds information from childhood, does the picking. Hence, we pick someone who has qualities similar to those of our parents, both positive and negative, and our partner does the same. For example, maybe your partner's mom was overly critical, and you also have this tendency. Perhaps your dad was emotionally unavailable, and your husband can also be distant. Our subconscious mind intentionally seeks someone who can help activate our unresolved trauma so it can surface for healing.

To develop a secure attachment style, we are required to develop consciousness and communication in our relationships. When we feel upset with our partner, instead of falling into patterns of blame and judgment, we must get curious about *why* we feel hurt and what *our* role is in the conflict. To do this, it can be helpful to identify what relationship dynamics from childhood are getting repeated. The goal is for each partner to become aware of how they trigger each other and to use the information to support their growth and healing.

Transforming our attachment style is a process with many layers. Here are simple strategies to support you in strengthening your sense of security in relationships.

- **Observe.** Notice when you feel insecure in relationships. If you are avoidant, you may feel more stressed when your partner is seeking connection or is emotionally distressed. If you are ambivalent, you can feel abandoned if your partner is withdrawn, quiet, or working a lot. If you are disorganized, you may feel intensely jealous if your partner is spending time with friends or coworkers. Pay attention to the types of scenarios that commonly activate feelings of insecurity.

- **Identify and communicate needs.** When you determine the types of behaviors in your partner that trigger you, identify your needs that are getting activated. If you're an avoidant adult, you may need sufficient alone time and for your partner to schedule time with you to discuss problems rather than springing them on you. If you are ambivalent, you may need quality time with your partner each day. If you are disorganized, you may need your partner to daily offer reassurance of love.

- **Self-soothe.** Healthy relationships involve balancing the ability to meet our own needs and receive support from our partner. Becoming secure involves increasing our ability to manage our own emotional state without expecting our partner to soothe us.

- **List your partner's assets.** My favorite tool for increasing feelings of connection between partners, regardless of attachment style, is to keep a journal dedicated to singing the praises of your partner. Each day make a list of your partner's good qualities and positive contributions to your life. Allow yourself to focus on your partner's strengths instead of deficiencies.

Our relationship template is determined by what we witnessed in our parents' relationship with each other, with non-intimate others, and with us. This template shows us what to expect from people, how to communicate, and how to interpret others' behaviors. Understanding our relationship template can help explain the quality of our current adult relationships. The problems we bring to our relationships do not reflect a fundamental flaw in us: They reflect what we have learned about relationships and how we protect ourselves. We are not stuck with this template if we are willing to do what it takes to heal. We are not meant to live in isolation. Learning to more intentionally and mindfully cultivate positive connections with others is instrumental to living a fulfilling life.

Chapter 5

Beliefs

W hat do you believe? Do you believe people are good and life is fun, or do you believe you can't trust others and life is hard? Do you believe some people are lucky in life, but good things don't happen to you? Do you believe you are worthy? Do you believe you matter? Do you believe you can heal?

Beliefs are powerful forces that dictate what we expect and experience in life. The experiences we have in our first relationships lay the foundation for what we believe. When interactions with caregivers are positive and loving, we believe the world is safe, people are good, and we are worthy. We develop what is known as a "positive internal working model." Equipped with positive beliefs, we develop a sense of confidence that allows us to easily engage in life in a way that leads to even more validating and positive experiences.

Negative beliefs are generated in response to life experiences for the purpose of survival. When the predominant way parents interact with children is negative, whether with neglect, control, or criticism, the children create belief structures that center on the expectation of harm. We develop a "negative internal working model" that can include beliefs such as "The world is dangerous" and "I can't trust the people in charge." Additionally, beliefs related to unworthiness take hold, such as "I am bad," "I am unlovable," "I am unworthy," and "It's my fault."

Learning more about the subconscious mind can help us understand how our early beliefs become dominant. I invite you to remember what it was like learning to drive a car. The initial stages involve thoughtfully and consciously taking many precautions to be safe and follow the rules of the road. The driving novice carefully buckles up, adjusts the mirrors, puts the car in Drive, and stops cautiously at stop signs and red lights. Once the driver has had enough practice, the patterns required to drive are dropped into the subconscious mind, allowing the processes involved to become automatic. This frees up the brain to engage in other activities necessary to promote survival, allowing for efficiency.

Beliefs work the same way.

For safety, it is important to be able to make predictions in life. Beliefs provide a shortcut. Once established, beliefs run automatically and no longer require conscious thought. For example, if children are hurt by men, they develop the belief that men are dangerous. The survival purpose of this belief is to motivate the cautious behavior deemed necessary to avoid further harm from men. After being shown that our voice doesn't matter as children, the belief that "nothing helps" emerges so we don't waste our energy on impossible goals. As an adult, however, these old beliefs limit what is possible.

Our original traumas are the primary source of our limiting beliefs. Though the details vary for each traumatized child, the core wounding is essentially the same: *abandonment*. Abandonment can be experienced by a premature infant spending the early days and weeks of life in the neonatal intensive care unit (NICU). The infant has no framework to understand that the disconnection from the warmth, comfort, and familiarity of parents is to help save their life. But even if the infant did understand, there is still no substitute for the physical and emotional warmth of a loving parent.

Abandonment can result from neglect when parents are high on drugs, work all the time, leave their child's life, or for whatever reason are inattentive and mis-attuned. Children can also feel a sense of abandonment when parents are angry, critical, and controlling. Regardless of the conditions associated with feeling abandoned, children conclude there is no one to truly depend upon.

The conditions of abandonment produce the survival beliefs that are most appropriate for our circumstances. A premature infant can develop the belief "I am helpless" as a result of being separated from their mother. Later in life this belief will lead to helpless behavior, the survival purpose of which is to elicit care from others. The neglected child will develop beliefs about feeling unimportant, unworthy, and all alone. The survival function of these beliefs is to stay small, preventing further rejection. When abused, we develop the belief we are not safe. The benefit of this belief is the emerging vigilance that helps us avoid more harm.

Beliefs are also inherited from our parents and ancestors, passed down in our DNA and absorbed from the environment in which we were raised. For example, a friend talked about his desire to clear blocks to financial abundance. As we discussed what he learned about money growing up, he realized he had unknowingly adopted his father's beliefs. He said they had the same pattern: the ability to easily make money, but the inability to hold on to it. I'm certain the litany of beliefs about helplessness that I stored were not only cultivated by my personal experiences of abuse and neglect but also absorbed from both my parents and likely from previous generations that also experienced various forms of trauma.

Our beliefs guide the way we relate to the world. They dictate how we think, feel, and behave.

I heard Dr. Bruce Perry, an expert on child trauma, describe an event he witnessed in an airport that illustrated how a child with a positive internal working model may respond to behavior that contradicts her positive expectations of life. A well-dressed businessman, angry about a flight delay, dramatically approached the customer service desk, insisting he was an important customer and had to immediately board the flight. Everyone waiting noticed a young girl, who appeared mesmerized by the man.

When he was refused, he huffed back to his seat, sat down, exasperated, and pulled out a newspaper to read. The young girl mischievously walked over to the man and playfully punched the paper. The businessman relaxed as the innocent young girl smiled at him, proud of herself, and continued to playfully engage with him as her parents carefully watched. By the time the plane was ready for boarding, the two had become buddies. Why? The young girl believed she was worthy of kindness and the man's irritability did not resonate with her internal working model, so she persistently and playfully coaxed him to behave in a way that aligned with her beliefs.

On the other hand, when children hold beliefs related to fear and unworthiness, the internal working model sets the stage for them to encounter further traumatic and destructive experiences throughout life. When our brain is fixated on a belief, it prevents us from seeing contradictory information. For example, people who believe they are unworthy will struggle to receive compliments.

Scenes from the animated movie *Meet the Robinsons* provide rich examples of a negative internal working model. Lewis lives in an orphanage, and after being rejected by more than two hundred potential parents, he invents a memory scanner to retrieve the memory of his mother so he can track her down.

The memory scanner does not work, and Lewis's internal working model convinces him it is because he is "no good," which he believes because of his history of abandonment and rejection. Lewis's roommate in the orphanage, Michael, is kept awake at night while Lewis works away on his memory scanner. Because Michael was tired, he missed a fly ball in a baseball game, and his team lost the league championship. In a flashback, the audience sees that although his teammates were unhappy with him, other kids still wanted to be his friend, inviting him to play. However, Michael believed he was unworthy and unwanted, and saw only what he believed: that everyone hated him.

Beliefs can turn into identities. An identity is the persona one adopts that is associated with roles in life. Before my health breakdown, I was a successful therapist. I was regularly approached to give workshops to teach parents and professionals how to help kids with attachment disorder. I had a professional identity of confidence and competence. In contrast, my identity as a wife and mother was less solid. I constantly questioned my capabilities and struggled with depression. I routinely felt I was missing the mark and was very hard on myself, constantly comparing myself with others and convincing myself I was never a good enough wife and mother.

Why the discrepancy between work and home? Our identities are often based on what we experience in our childhood environment. I received recognition from my parents only was when I was successful. Achieving academic success and having athletic wins was the only time I felt my parents were pleased with me. Although their acceptance was temporary, I quickly equated success with worthiness. This primed my professional identity of competency. However, to some degree, my identity as a wife and mother was based on what my parents modeled: They were depressed, impatient, anxious, irritable, and never pleased.

Like it or not, they were my role models. Until I healed myself, being a depressed wife and mom was a skin I could not shed. My depressed persona at home eventually dissolved. By healing myself, I accessed my true self, which allowed me to naturally be a more loving, patient, confident, and gentle wife and mother. I also developed a good sense of humor and now regularly amuse myself and sometimes others with how funny I can be.

When I began to more fully understand the relationship between beliefs and problems in life, I became more curious about the unconscious beliefs at play when life was not going smoothly for me. I started routinely asking myself, *What is really bothering me?* It became clear that one repeated cause of distress was the belief "I am completely on my own." If I or a loved one was facing a challenge, I believed it was entirely up to me to get us through it. This belief developed in childhood because it was true then. I had to face enormous hardship on my own; there were no adults who protected me, and everything was a struggle. The protective purpose of the belief "I am completely on my own" was to motivate me to take care of myself. If I had held the expectation that I could depend on others, I may not have survived. However, this belief was no longer necessary in adulthood, and it caused much unnecessary suffering.

Though insight is helpful when it comes to uncovering limiting beliefs, understanding alone is not enough to shift deeply held ones. In fact, some beliefs can take substantial effort to release. It has taken years for me to shift beliefs related to safety, because of extensive evidence supporting my lack of safety. Though I feel more and more safe all the time, I still can have trauma responses in reaction to nonthreatening stimuli. Each time this happens, it reveals another layer of trauma to address.

One way to uncover beliefs is to take an honest look at your life. Our current life circumstances reflect the beliefs we hold. How are your relationships? Do you feel socially isolated? Perhaps you hold beliefs that you are not likable or that relationships are too much trouble. Maybe you believe men, or women, don't stick around. Are you not as financially successful as you would like to be? You may believe you are destined to be poor or that money is the root of all evil. At the heart of unwanted life experiences is a set of survival-based beliefs that govern us. Without awareness, our limiting beliefs constantly operate in the background, bringing more hardship.

When we release a limiting belief, the falsity is gone and the truth emerges. By releasing the belief "I am unworthy," for example, we return to present time and simply know we *are* worthy. It is not necessary, nor is it particularly helpful, to drill ourselves with positive affirmations to compel a shift in beliefs. I worked with a client who was going through a devastating breakup. Her husband was leaving her, which activated memories of abandonment by her dad, who left the family when she was five. We worked to clear the belief "I'm all alone." At the conclusion of the work, she readily declared with certainty, "I'm not alone, I have a lot of people supporting me." This profound shift allowed her to move through her grief more rapidly.

Clearing limiting beliefs often requires us to heal the original wounds responsible for creating them. Many healing methods can effectively help us heal trauma and the limiting beliefs associated with our unhealed pain. Trauma therapy like EMDR, Somatic Experiencing, Logosynthesis, and the Emotional Freedom Technique (EFT) can be helpful. Hypnotherapy and energy healing modalities can also help resolve trauma and limiting beliefs. Descriptions of these treatment methods can be found in the appendix.

Developmental trauma is complex. Children must somehow navigate chronically complicated, confusing, and painful interactions with parents. Our mind uses beliefs to help us select precise strategies for navigating difficulties. Therefore, the purpose of beliefs is protective, as survival requires us to efficiently respond to danger. Although this can be helpful in childhood, the beliefs that once protected us can seriously limit our lives as adults when we are no longer in danger. Fortunately, the brain is malleable, and though the beliefs that make up the internal working model are rigid, they are also changeable.

Chapter 6

A Template for Abuse

Being on the receiving end of abuse can be horrific. I have deep compassion for anyone who has been hurt by others. Recovery can be arduous and extensive. Complicating matters, people who are victimized are often blamed for their abuse. Rape and domestic violence victims are often perceived with skepticism, as though they caused or could have prevented the attacks on them. Women are often sized up by appearance, alcohol use, and sexual history and held accountable for the criminal behavior of others. Men who have been assaulted also often have their experiences minimized and can be told they are lucky if they are sexually violated.

The story of Chanel Miller, who was assaulted by a Stanford student in 2015, illustrates how, with clear and compelling evidence, our society still struggles to hold abusers accountable. In her case, two graduate students found Chanel unconscious, with her attacker on top of her. He was given a shockingly light sentence despite substantial evidence, while Chanel spent years navigating both her trauma and an unjust justice system, which clearly was more sympathetic toward an elite athlete-perpetrator than toward his victim.

When someone is victimized, it is never their fault. When abuse occurs, a crime has been committed and the violator should be held accountable. This is not debatable. However, in addition to assigning responsibility to the abuser, important questions must be asked to understand *why* the abuse happened.

What occurred in the perpetrator's life that led them to become a victimizer? Did this person feel loved and safe growing up? Was this person taught to respect the rights and boundaries of others?

We must not confine our investigation into the cause of abuse to the perpetrator. If we do, we seriously limit our understanding about the culpability of our society, which is also a guilty party. It is exceedingly important to uncover variables at play in society where extensive and pervasive abuse is allowed because we have yet to acknowledge the fact that trauma is rampant. Without understanding societal contributions to abusive behavior, it is impossible for our culture to move toward more safety and respect for all people.

In our culture, no one is spared the experience of trauma. For many of us, it starts when we are born into an overwhelming environment filled with loud noises, bright lights, and separation from our mother that often prioritizes the physical body over emotional needs. The experience of trauma and disconnection from self continues through exposure to the many institutions that insist that children conform to what is acceptable instead of being allowed creative freedom and individuality. Trauma is perpetuated when wounded parents pass on their pain to their children, who then pass on their pain to other children. Wounded people in positions of authority pass on their pain by abusing their power over subordinates; because these people also serve as societal role models, their behavior seemingly gives others permission to mistreat vulnerable people. There are many ways a person can be hurt in this world; it largely stems from the behavior of people with unhealed wounds who are not in touch with their Essence.

To live an empowered life we must be aware that wounding is a necessary part of learning and growth in our human experience. After we have been wounded, part of our growth relies on our ability to explore how we can reduce our vulnerability to more abuse. Ideally, we would not be required to be mindful of how to keep ourselves safe. The society many of us dream of would allow us all to be free of harm and free to be ourselves. Until humanity reaches a more enlightened state, though, it is important for each of us to assess how we can limit the likelihood of being victimized. Identifying our template of abuse is one important way we can address the wounds that make us vulnerable.

Each person with unhealed trauma unknowingly engages in scenarios resembling earlier unresolved traumatic experiences. This is known as *trauma reenactment*. They occur as the result of our template of abuse, which contains the damaging conclusions we have made about ourselves, life, and others. It's the fear-based narrative we unconsciously tell ourselves that guides us toward hardship. For example, if our parents were undependable, our trauma narrative is *I can't depend on others.* We then unconsciously prove ourselves right by associating with people who let us down. If we were unseen, we believe we don't matter and then verify this belief by creating experiences where we feel invisible. When we experience hardship, it is often because our subconscious mind is simply following the limiting beliefs developed during our troubled youth. We will continue to reexperience elements of our traumas until we update our belief system, notifying it through our trauma healing that the past is over.

Many people suffer with guilt and shame after abuse because they feel responsible for what happened to them. This self-blame is misplaced when we unnecessarily take responsibility for the abuser's behavior. Some inner torment relates to our knowing that we could have done more to keep ourselves safe.

We may know using alcohol prevented us from identifying the negative intentions of others. We may realize that the desire to be wanted caused us to ignore the red flags. We could have struggled to set boundaries because we could not access our voice. We also could have engaged in risky behavior because we wanted to feel alive. What propels us to put ourselves in harm's way? To a large degree, it is our template of abuse.

To transform our abuse template, traumatic experiences from childhood must be brought into consciousness so they can be examined, explored, understood, and healed. Healing our original wounds allows us to release the trauma-related beliefs and coping mechanisms that disable us. We cannot control the free will of others; therefore, healing our trauma is the most effective remedy to ending re-victimization. This makes us less of a magnet for those with threatening intentions.

I'm sharing examples from my own childhood to illustrate how the psyche of an abused child contributes to trauma reenactments. If you have a history of sexual trauma, please be sure you are well supported if needed when you read this section. Please take good care of yourself and read at a pace that feels right to you.

It was not just my dad who sexually abused me. I also experienced a series of sexual violations from older boys. Without question, the extensive abuse I experienced in my family laid the groundwork for further abuse, but at the time I didn't understand why I was such a target for sexual victimizers.

First was the older boy in the park who was deemed cool by the elementary school kids because he had a moped. He was an attraction for the kids whose parents were in the bleachers, watching baseball games.

Like many other kids, one day I went to the area of the park where he was offering rides. While waiting my turn, I was unexpectedly summoned to the front of the line. This teenager had quickly identified me as his target. Predators are eerily able to spot a seasoned victim, probably because they have also been victimized and unknowingly see themselves in the wounded prey they seek.

I accepted my fast pass and went ahead of the kids who had been waiting in line, but I felt confused. I did not know him and was uncertain why I was given special treatment. I noticed my reservations but paid more attention to enjoying feeling special. I ignored my internal alarm because my hunger to feel wanted, chosen, and important was intense. Feeling special was a rare and cherished occurrence. In those initial moments, that was all I cared about. I got on the moped with him, and he took off.

He usually rode around the park in a predictable route, so when he strayed from his typical path, the fear I had been suppressing about being in close contact with him became palpable. I just wanted to be back at the park with my friends, away from what felt like impending doom. Farther away from the crowd, he made his move. He put his hand on my pelvis and said, "Do you want to lay me?" Instantly, I froze. I had never heard those words before, but I knew precisely what he meant. I pretended not to hear him to buy time. He repeated himself and steered the moped farther away from anyone who could help, but fortunately, his plan was thwarted. As he was forced to bring the moped to a halt at a stop sign, I somehow got off the bike and headed quickly toward the safety of the park.

It is the strangest thing to so desperately want comfort but to be terrified of the person from whom you need support. By this time, I was an experienced suppresser. It did not even occur to me to tell my parents or anyone else what happened.

My mother had already shown me that she was incapable of protecting me or comforting me. I was well versed with the protocol: Be used and harmed, suck it up, stuff it. No one cares and no one will help you. This was my template of abuse.

The second assault outside my family occurred in high school. A common activity on the weekends was to gather with classmates and drink alcohol. We drank at older kids' homes and partied in the country. We numbed ourselves and giggled, and it was a relief to be away from the dominance of my parents. I imagine the alcohol was the only thing that relieved the relentless anxiety that persistently reminded me never to let my guard down. Unfortunately, there can be consequences to the reduced hypervigilance associated with alcohol or other drugs.

Alcohol allows us to be less conscious of our pain. Yes, it can be fun to drink and to have reduced inhibitions, but the cost can be high. Intoxication makes our awareness go off-line, making it impossible to fully and intentionally manage our own thoughts, behaviors, and reactions. When we use alcohol and drugs, we contribute to our own vulnerability by removing the one thing we can control: ourselves. This leaves a door open for other wounded people to take advantage.

During one of the weekend parties when I was sixteen, I was told that Shawn (not his real name) was interested in me. This felt like an unlikely pairing. I was a good girl, always striving for the approval of others. Shawn was popular but had a reputation for using illicit substances much more taboo than alcohol. Exhausted from being the good girl and allured by the stereotypical bad boy, I was intrigued, and agreed to date this person who was entirely wrong for me.

We did not actually go on dates, but we hung out at parties. I would sneak out of my house, and he would pick me up.

We would talk for hours. I did not know that we were very similarly wounded people. In retrospect, I believe he had his own sexual trauma, so he had confusing ideas about sex and relationships. One night he did not respect my boundaries and I was sexually violated. It was unexpected and traumatizing. I abruptly ended all contact with him. He didn't understand. Confused and internally conflicted myself, I told my friends I still cared about him. Considering that, one friend questioned if I had actually been sexually assaulted. I was full of shame and self-blame. Having no idea how to sort this out, I suppressed it, too, falling even deeper into a state of self-loathing and distrust of life.

My teenage years were brutal. I had so much internal rage toward my parents and feared them, yet I still deeply wanted their love, approval, and affection. It was a true cocktail of nearly unbearable pain. This is when my suicidal thoughts really began mounting. It is a wonder I made it through.

My third experience of sexual assault outside my family happened after I left my house following a fight with my parents. I did not want to feel, think, or even live. I went to a party and drank alcohol to numb myself. Intoxicated, I again was in a vulnerable situation, and one of my best friends sexually violated me. I was in and out of consciousness while it was happening and was simultaneously shocked, confused, and just plain sad. The next morning, I was in disbelief. My friend meant a lot to me, so I called him, hoping for a good explanation or that he would apologize. Instead, I was gaslighted: He denied that anything had happened.

My abuse template centered on the expectation of betrayal, which put me at terrible risk of being further victimized. When children do not receive the attention, validation, and connection required to fulfill basic needs, they will crave it endlessly. At times, they will do anything to receive attention and love, including dismissing their own need for safety, and unconsciously trade affection for abuse.

Re-traumatization also happens because of defensive mechanisms that once protected us. Conditioned to cope by using denial and numbing, we may not recognize the signs of danger and therefore lack the consciousness to object to mistreatment. Additionally, our conditioned freeze response prevents healthy access to our fight-or-flight response, often rendering us incapable of advocating for ourselves.

In all cases where I was sexually assaulted, I believe those who violated me were traumatized people. For decades, I solely blamed them for the abuse. What I have learned, however, is this conclusion ignores the bigger picture, which is necessary to grasp to end victimization. If we only blame the perpetrator, it limits the responsibility of our society at large that continues to ignore our needs for unconditional love, acceptance, and safety. We all have a fundamental need to be seen, heard, and respected not just by our families, but by humanity.

When we have been harmed, we have a choice about how to navigate the aftermath. We can maintain the powerlessness that was initiated by the violence, or we can use the unwanted experience to fuel recovery and personal growth. To live an empowered life, we must take responsibility for healing our trauma. Transcending trauma requires us to understand *how* our own history of wounding and the resulting coping methods put us in vulnerable situations that allow more trauma to occur.

Ending our own pattern of being victimized requires us to take an inventory of why we were vulnerable. We must take personal responsibility for identifying how our abuse template led to trauma reenactments. Personal responsibility is true self-protection. Acknowledging how our abuse template contributes to unwanted experiences allows us to empower and protect ourselves. This requires a high level of self-awareness and commitment to moving beyond the perception of victimization.

When you are ready, and preferably with the guidance of a trauma-informed helping professional, it can be helpful to become clearer about your own template of abuse and its impact on your life. Below are questions to assist you in uncovering the thoughts, beliefs, and expectations that can put you at risk of being harmed by another person and help you better understand yourself. Your responses can clarify your abuse template by helping to expose limiting beliefs and dangerous patterns of behavior. You may uncover ways you unknowingly feel helpless or are naively dependent on others. Uncovering your trauma narrative takes time and happens in layers, so consider revisiting these questions on a regular basis. As your healing journey deepens, it becomes easier to more objectively understand yourself, your reactions, and your patterns.

- What do I expect from life?
- What do I expect from relationships?
- What do I think of myself?
- How do people treat me?
- How do I treat others?
- How do I get my needs met?
- How do I protect myself?
- Do I feel victimized by life?
- Do I put myself in situations where I am vulnerable to abuse?
- What current experiences in my life resemble negative experiences from my childhood?

- What is the story I tell myself when someone says or does something I don't like?
- Where do I give my power away and why?
- Can I set boundaries? With whom is it more difficult to set boundaries, and why?

Identifying your trauma narrative is empowering. It is necessary for people who truly want to take responsibility for themselves and consciously create a fulfilling life. It requires mindfulness, self-awareness, and willingness to see the uncomfortable truth about how your template of abuse has put you in harm's way. We all live with some degree of anesthesia, which puts us at risk of being victimized until we do the necessary work to raise our consciousness and see our life with more clarity. Choosing to live intentionally and consciously can allow you to become more empowered and capable of transforming your abuse template into one that aligns you with the possibility of a joyful and fulfilling life.

Chapter 7

How We Cope

We are meant to live life as our true self. Ideally, we feel free to assert ourselves to meet our needs, ask others to support us, and set limits when necessary. When caregivers are attuned and respond lovingly to children's requests, children feel safe and develop confidence in themselves and others. Additionally, when parents set limits with love, it teaches children that it's safe to ask for what they want, no matter the outcome. This teaches them to have courage and helps them learn to handle disappointment. This way of parenting promotes a sense of personal power and allows children to stay more closely connected to their Essence.

In contrast, when children cannot depend on parents to respond to their needs with kindness, it is painful and alarming. Fear removes the freedom of playfulness, curiosity, and assertiveness. To cope, we develop strategies to insulate ourselves from feeling the intensity of situations we are not built to easily withstand. These strategies protect us from the pain of the original insult and increase the likelihood of our safety. For example, children raised by controlling parents can be less harmed when they cope by giving up their voice. Children who are overly helpful may be assured they have a meal to eat if they become the cook. The downside of protective mechanisms is that we lose who we are. Being ourselves is a luxury we cannot afford when we are in danger.

This chapter addresses many of the common adaptations children use to avoid feeling the pain of physical abuse, rejection, invisibility, and criticism from parents. I invite you to notice how you have used or continue to use these coping strategies. While doing so, please suspend judgment of yourself. These tools offered you relief in childhood when life was overwhelming. In some cases, we truly would not have survived without them. The key is to recognize that what served you in childhood could be limiting or harming you now. When you continue to numb yourself in the various ways that people trying to avoid pain do, you prevent yourself from facing your original wounds and instead create more problems.

Dissociation

Dissociation is the process of disconnecting from ourselves as the result of overwhelming emotional or physical pain. It is a psychological tool allowing us to disengage when we feel alone, ashamed, or shocked and the resulting internal state is unbearable. For emotional protection, the brain prevents us from being fully present when we are traumatized, but that leaves trauma unprocessed.

Dissociation is apparent when a person suddenly appears vacant, or simply "not there." People often do not know they are dissociating, but others may joke, "Hey, where did you go?" or snap their fingers while saying, "Are you in there?" Someone with developmental trauma may easily fall into this state during even minor stressful situations. When we dissociate, we can unknowingly be emotionally and mentally absent when we must be present. Dissociation can be a fleeting state for adults, but those who are more severely traumatized can exist in a chronic state of dissociation where they live in a frozen state, barely engaged in life. Dissociation is the foundational state for the other methods of coping described here. When children and adults are people pleasing, self-harming, suppressing, perfectionistic, and avoiding, you can know they are also in a dissociated state and disconnected from Essence.

People Pleasing

Children have a way of easily discovering what pleases and displeases parents, especially when parents are troubled. Under these circumstances, children develop "spidey" senses to identify how to best increase the likelihood of safety and reduce the likelihood of rejection. This pleasing behavior is also referred to as fawning. Many people know that fight, flight, and freeze are options when under threat of attack. However, fawning has been referred to as the fourth *f* with regard to survival responses. Pete Walker, author of *Complex PTSD: From Surviving to Thriving*, says that people who use a fawning survival style "seek safety by merging with the wishes, needs, and demands of others. They act as if they believe that the price of admission to any relationship is the forfeiture of all their needs, rights, preferences, and boundaries" (p. 122).

I see two primary parenting dynamics that produce people pleasers. One is the result of being raised by helpless parents. When parents are needy, it scares children. Helpless parents can over-rely on their children for companionship and caring for siblings. These expectations are inappropriate and put kids at risk for prematurely feeling and behaving like an adult. When parents are overwhelmed, dependent, and depressed, many kids suppress their needs to prevent burdening them. People-pleasing behavior becomes a coping strategy to help increase a sense of safety by limiting the demands placed on those who lack the resiliency to respond in a way that feels good. People pleasing also occurs in these situations because children truly care about their parents and want to help.

The second cause of people-pleasing behavior is being raised by angry, critical, and unpredictable parents. Parents who are demanding create fear and even terror in children. Under these conditions, children work to please parents to avoid emotional and physical violence. These children become adept at studying cues from parents to predict negative moods and adjust their own needs and behaviors. This is an incredibly stressful way to live.

Pleasing in childhood can be dangerous. Even some well-meaning parents believe teaching their children to obey is the way to raise "good" children. However, when as children we do not learn to think for ourselves, we are conditioned to do what we are told by people in positions of power. We do not learn to make decisions for ourselves and will often participate in a variety of damaging experiences because we simply do not realize we have a choice and feel the only way to feel safe and worthy is to comply and please, regardless of the personal cost.

Society loves a people pleaser. Many people are happy to benefit from the extensive generosity of a person with this tendency. Adults routinely praise people who "always put others first." However, the cost of pleasing others can be quite high as it can lead to sacrificing needs for personal time, family time, eating, and sleeping. Dr. Gabor Maté, author of *When the Body Says No*, says prioritizing the needs of others over our own is a major risk factor for disease. It also puts us at risk for abuse and exploitation.

In our work together, Kelsey talked about how she was raised to please others. As the only daughter in a conservative family, she was taught it was her duty to set aside her own needs and make others happy by caring for her siblings and helping substantially with housework. As a young adult, Kelsey was sexually assaulted by an acquaintance. She told me she felt she did not have the right to say no because she was taught to please others, despite the cost to her. In addition, she married someone who contributes very little to the high demands of raising children and managing the household. She initiated therapy because of depression. She told me, "I was trained to be a good girl and to take care of others. I don't even know who I am."

In my own experience of people pleasing, I made a big shift after I realized it can lead to irritability. I mentioned to a life coach that I could be cranky with my husband and children at times, without understanding why. My coach said that not setting boundaries because of my tendency to over-function can lead to resentment. In working with many adults who also over-function to please others, it became clear that we do not want our children to feel devalued like we did, so we overcompensate by doing too much for them. Parents who over-function can not only develop resentment but also raise children who are helpless to meet their own needs. Instead of becoming independent, confident adults, they can develop the expectation that others will take care of them. The desire to raise empowered children is a good motivator to shift out of this pattern.

Suppression and Denial

When life is difficult for children, and they cannot escape, they learn to suppress unmanageable thoughts, feelings, wants, and needs to avoid overwhelming emotional pain. They create a false narrative, known as denial, to therapeutically pretend life is not so bad. As traumatized children, we still need our parents and must convince ourselves that they are better than they are, so we can cope. We may tell ourselves, *It's my fault my mom got so mad; I was bad*, or *My dad didn't mean it*, or *My mom was just having a bad day*. The partnership forged between suppression and denial allows us to feel less emotional pain and to sustain, as much as possible, a connection with our limited parent.

Suppression and denial persisting into adulthood become problematic. These coping skills can lead to further instances of mistreatment because we have been conditioned to allow others, especially people in positions of power, to dominate us. When we are trained to suppress uncomfortable emotions and to dismiss the misbehavior of others, it prevents us from being able to access our own power and stand up for ourselves. Traumatized adults both suppress emotions that could have notified them of a boundary violation and deny they have the power to protect themselves. Many adults convince themselves "It's not that bad," just like they did in childhood.

Self-Abuse

A client once told me, "Being my own worst enemy protects me." Many children feel that if given a choice, self-harm is preferential to harm by parents. Children can believe if they beat parents to the punch, so to speak, parents may hurt them less, and so they criticize themselves, limit their potential, and have poor self-care. Self-abuse can also serve as a gesture of loyalty to abusive parents. Many traumatized children and adults feel they cannot be more capable, successful, or happy than their parents, so they stay small. This occurs when parents have the attitude "If you aren't with me, you are against me." Children may also use self-punishing methods to "keep themselves in line." In these cases, self-abuse is used by children to coerce themselves into perfection to prevent the errors that could lead to abuse. In these cases, children can engage in self-punishment for making "mistakes," feeling "weak," wanting things they cannot have, or even for simply existing.

In adulthood, self-abuse shows itself in the words people use, such as "I am such an idiot," I can't do anything right," and "I suck at life." It also is expressed in behaviors such as cutting, substance abuse, socializing with or having sex with uncaring people, and self-deprecating behaviors such as making themselves the butt of jokes. Patterns of self-demeaning behavior beginning in childhood become automatic by adulthood.

I asked Laila, a smart and insightful business professional, why she thought she did not love herself. She was at a total loss to explain to herself or me why she was so full of self-abuse with her eating disorder, self-criticism, and lack of self-care. As we explored the origin of her critical view of herself, it became clear to her that this behavior was a programmed way of treating herself based on the messages she received in childhood. She felt like a failure as a kid, condemned herself for it, and maintained the self-loathing behavior as an adult. Learning to love herself required incredible discipline, which was motivated by a heartfelt desire to be a loving mother to her children.

Perfectionism

Abuse breeds perfectionism. Children work hard to win the approval and dodge the rejection and disdain of parents who consistently give them the message that they are not good enough. Children can then torment themselves in their pursuit of eliminating mistakes. In some cases, children may avoid some harm by trying to be perfect. For others, even near perfection is not good enough.

Being programmed for perfectionism in childhood leads to perfectionistic adults who develop a compulsion toward achievement. We tend to associate our worth with accomplishment, whether it is advancement at work or completing household tasks effectively. Perfectionistic adults are often unknowingly searching for the approval from others that they longed for from parents. However, because the need for approval is only a symptom of trauma, achievements and accomplishments can never fill the void of feeling unloved and unworthy.

Keesha shared with me that one night she was putting her infant daughter to bed, and the process was not going smoothly. Her husband offered his help, which she thought was critical of her parenting. We explored why she reflexively drew this conclusion. After thinking it through, she said achieving excellence was the only way she could receive approval from her parents. As a child she became driven to excel in every area of her life because her parents believed average was not good enough. This template convinced her that rejection was imminent if her behavior was anything less than perfect, even when it came to putting her child to bed.

Avoidance

When parents have clearly demonstrated they are undependable, children can become highly self-reliant. This coping style is avoidance; it is an attempt to reduce the pain of having unmet needs. Children withdraw to curb feelings of abandonment. They numb themselves to turn off desires, convincing themselves they don't need what they are actually desperate to receive. Many adults who cope using avoidance are seasoned at not noticing problems. They are unlikely to acknowledge that their childhood was painful. They avoid conflicts with everyone to limit vulnerability. However, most adults who routinely use avoidance to cope remain acutely aware of their loneliness. We can feel paralyzed and grief-stricken when what we fear the most, connection, is also what we most want.

It is essential to understand that how we cope with adversity as kids is also how we cope as adults. The coping tools from childhood are "cut-and-pasted" into adulthood. To have wellness, we must be intentional, mindful, and conscious of how and why we respond to people and life situations the way we do. When we are not intentional, we are simply running the programs installed during a turbulent childhood. Coping patterns from childhood can seriously jeopardize health and well-being when adults consistently set aside their own needs in the case of people pleasing, become extreme workaholics in the case of perfectionism, or ignore serious health symptoms in the case of denial. Cycle breakers choose to live life intentionally, which requires healing what caused us to "cope" instead of living life to the fullest, in touch with our Essence.

Part II
CONSEQUENCES

The Enduring Impact of Childhood Trauma

O ur Essence knows how to be in the flow and how to embrace all of life, allowing us to reflect a state of health, peace, and positive expectation. Connection to our spiritual self enables us to be intentional with our thoughts, emotions, and behaviors. Our Essence is not limited by fear, the need for approval, or addictions. These are responses to life that reflect separation from Essence, which is inevitable with trauma.

When we grow up unsafe, we put forth our best attempt to self-protect and survive using a variety of tools. Suppression allowed us to believe life wasn't as bad as it was. People pleasing helped us stay on our parents' good side as much as possible. Perfectionism may have helped eliminate mistakes, preventing punishment. We hang on to beliefs and strategies that seemed to work, whether or not we still need them.

However, operating from fear-based survival strategies can unnecessarily perpetuate our trauma as adults. Our trauma-informed templates can become like dictators, guiding our thoughts, emotions, and behaviors without taking into consideration how our adult life is different from childhood. The consequences can be massive. Thoughts can be intrusive and compel us to expect hardship. Emotions can rapidly and unexpectedly take us to dark places. Our behavior can be destructive to ourselves and others. Our bodies, which will not stop keeping score, reflect the accumulated pain we have suffered. Triggers can feel like frequent ambushes.

Unhealed developmental trauma can impact every aspect of our life, making trauma symptoms unpreventable. Whereas some children and adults with a secure upbringing can experience a traumatic event and bounce back, trauma that happens in childhood, leaving kids feeling unsafe and unworthy, is much more likely to have an enduring effect.

My goal is to de-shame symptoms that emerge from the fallout of childhood trauma. Instead of judging ourselves and others for anxiety, fear of rejection, and codependency, for example, it is more helpful to understand how and why these symptoms emerged. When we more fully understand why we think, feel, and behave the way we do, it is easier to both generate compassion for ourselves and have the motivation it takes to bring healing to ourselves.

The chapters in Part II explain many consequences of a difficult childhood. I invite you to notice how any of the trauma patterns described here are reflected in your life. Be gentle with yourself as you do so. Please realize we cannot change what we do not see, and we cannot heal when we feel shame. Your complicated patterns of dealing with life are normal reactions to painful and complicated circumstances. They emerged to help you adapt to hardship and persist into adulthood because part of you still believes you are not safe.

Chapter 8

Triggers

*T*rigger is now a household word, embraced by society as an indicator of personal distress. I joked with my adult daughter recently that her messy teenage bedroom really triggered me when she was in middle school. However, she had no memory of the disarray. It reminded me that at the time, my need for control and order made it difficult for me to tolerate her comfort with disorder. To be honest, I still like order. A lot.

We are all triggered. Every day. Usually many times. A trigger is anything that takes us away from our peace. Feeling annoyed, angry, sad, and frustrated are signals we have been triggered. There are endless possibilities for what can trigger us. Some triggers are small and lead to mild emotional discomfort, like feeling guilty when we notice our plants need watering. Other triggers can evoke a stronger reaction, perhaps when our children are fighting, someone cuts us off in traffic, or our partner seems too friendly with a coworker.

Triggers are reminders of our unhealed traumas that have been waiting to be felt and addressed. When we are triggered, we blindly think, feel, and behave compulsively, automatically responding to a past stimulus we can't readily see. Triggers are personalized; we each have our own set of trauma reminders based on our specific wounds. What triggers one person may not trigger someone else.

Our triggers reveal our values, beliefs, and needs. Parents who value a positive and loving relationship with their children can be triggered when they angrily overreact to their children's behavior, which could activate beliefs about inadequacy. An employee who values accomplishment and praise, yet believes she is a failure, may feel triggered when it's time for her annual evaluation. A man who feels he needs his husband's presence and affection to feel worthy may feel triggered when his partner is withdrawn. Someone with the belief "I don't trust that my needs will be met" may be triggered by unexpected bills.

A popular saying in both the scientific and mental health communities helps illuminate why we get triggered: "What fires together, wires together." It means that once two experiences occur simultaneously, particularly when there is repetition or strong emotion, the presence of one of the variables will automatically activate the other. If your mom screamed at you for spilling a glass of milk, spilled milk became wired with fear. Therefore, as an adult, you will automatically feel afraid or angry if you or someone else spills a glass of milk— or anything else, for that matter. Pairing a stimulus (spilled milk) and a response (punishment) is a safety mechanism our brain uses to help prepare us for danger by carefully identifying potential threats based on past threats we have experienced. As a child, you may have become much more cautious when drinking milk after being harshly scolded, to avoid another attack. This is a benefit of triggers: When necessary, they can mobilize us to prepare for danger.

As an undergraduate student, I was in a psychology class one day when the topic of discussion was the validity of memory. As an experiment, our teacher had a fellow teaching assistant barge into the classroom in a disguise, playfully spray students with a squirt gun, and then quickly leave. The purpose was to later challenge us with how accurate our memories were regarding what we had witnessed. However, there was a war veteran in our class. Startled by this intrusion, he burst out of his seat and threw a chair across the room. His trigger was the unexpected ambush, and the reaction was terror. This was an innocent prank, but when it comes to survival, our brain does not take chances. That veteran's brain associated an ambush with the threat of death and produced an immediate fight-or-flight response, forcing him to act first and think later.

Though uncomfortable, triggers benefit our personal growth. James initiated therapy to address anger and irritability. A few months later his ailing mother came to live with him and his wife. She had been neglectful throughout his childhood, allowing his stepfather to regularly berate him. She also accompanied her truck driver husband on long trips, leaving James and his brother to fend for themselves at a young age.

In therapy, we identified how his mom's presence in his home triggered him. We then used this information to guide our trauma work. He told me he was triggered because he felt his mom frequently ignored him, but he wasn't sure if it was intentional or the result of dementia. As we explored this, James got in touch with a childhood memory of being ignored. He recalled how his mother often sat in a chair drinking coffee and completely neglected her children. This made James feel like he did not matter. We used Logosynthesis to address this memory and its accompanying belief. Afterward, James reported feeling much less triggered by both past and present instances of being ignored. Using the current trigger as the catalyst, James healed a layer of his childhood trauma, which made his daily life more comfortable.

As all parents know, raising children creates an uncountable number of triggering opportunities. One day I sent the following text to my husband as a joke and as an act of exasperation from being triggered by my teenage daughters: "Is it possible for parents to have a sabbatical?" The reply to my text was "Uh, wrong person." I had accidentally sent the text to my daughter instead of my husband. Oopsie. But the last laugh was on me. A few years later I googled my daughter when I was helping her prepare for her college admission applications and found she had shared the screenshot of our text exchange on Twitter.

Parenting is especially challenging for traumatized people because of the various ways children innocently trigger our unresolved pain. Many adults I see begin therapy after becoming parents because they don't want to repeat their parents' mistakes. Children and teens are notoriously demanding, resistant, and argumentative because these can be important qualities for individuation. However, these challenging behaviors may remind parents of how our own parents mistreated us, leading us to angrily lash out at our children or become passive to avoid conflict and tension. We parents can also feel triggered when we see our kids repeating our patterns and as a result feel shame and guilt because we know they learned them from us.

Freya is a single mom who had been committed to personal growth since her son was two. The love between them was a joy to witness. Freya once discussed with me her concern about how demanding and rigid she had become with him when he turned seven. To understand why this angry behavior had emerged, we explored what happened when she was seven: She lived with her grandmother, an abusive dictator. Freya realized she was experiencing a trauma reenactment with her son, becoming a less hostile version of her grandmother as her son mirrored her own wounded seven-year-old self, who felt alone and scared. This realization allowed Freya to bring healing to her own inner seven-year-old, which helped her change how she related to her son.

When a trigger comes from an interaction with another

person, it is known as *mirroring*. Mirroring is happening all the time. Life is always reflecting us to ourselves. In the mirroring process other people reflect our own hidden-to-us qualities, known as our *shadow*. Our shadow is the part of us we reject, ignore, dismiss, and deny. Shadow qualities reflect our unhealed pain, such as jealousy, bossiness, insecurity, arrogance, and dismissiveness. We often reject these parts of ourselves, thereby ignoring our wounds. Because these attributes are hidden to us, sometimes the only way we can see them is to project them onto others. For example, we might feel reactive to someone who is insecure because of our own insecurity. We may feel annoyed with someone who excessively complains because of our own negativity, and we may call out others who are addicts because we secretly feel ashamed of our addictions.

Observing others can teach us about mirroring. One way to do this is to watch reality TV. My family likes to watch the television show *Survivor*. It gives approximately twenty people the opportunity to see who can outwit, outlast, and outplay one another to win one million dollars. Inevitably, there is friction among players. Each season, reactivity occurs between players because they are very similar. One player may complain about another player for being bossy and controlling, not listening, or being lazy, but in most cases, the criticizing person has the same characteristic.

Mirrors can reflect our shadow traits and also mimic the behavior of those who hurt us. Although Joan longed to have a loving partnership with her husband, she found herself feeling irritated when he became depressed. She felt powerless and angry when he isolated himself. Through our work, she recognized that her husband was mirroring her father's depressive behavior. Her father was often depressed and distant, leaving her confused and scared as a child. With this insight, Joan worked to heal her inner child and became more empowered, feeling more compassion and less judgment toward her husband.

Mirroring reveals what we have yet to heal. It also reflects our brilliance. When we admire and look up to others, we are also seeing our own qualities, even if they haven't been fully developed and realized. Who do you look up to? Is it possible you have the same qualities?

I am certain that you have been triggered by reading this book. Probably many times. Take some time and identify how you have been triggered. Notice any upsetting memories, emotions, or thoughts that were brought to light. You may also want to note how you responded when you were triggered. Did you suppress what surfaced? Did you judge yourself or someone else? Can you allow yourself to consider that what triggered you is a road map containing the information you need to heal yourself? Are you willing to explore the values, needs, and unhealed trauma at the heart of your triggers?

We have choices when we are triggered: We can feel like a victim or respond productively. When we are ready to take responsibility for our lives, responding mindfully to triggers becomes empowering. Instead of blaming others for our unhappiness, we can use triggers to fuel healing. Carl Jung once said, "Everything that irritates us about others can lead us to an understanding of ourselves." Are you ready to understand yourself more fully? If so, please know triggers are your friend. Maybe they're not your best friend, but they're at least an acquaintance you can tolerate until it's time for you to part.

Chapter 9

Mental and Emotional Consequences

Many of us yearn for a way to simply delete unwanted thoughts and emotions. The gut-wrenching emotional pain and mental torment that comes with memories of betrayal and abandonment hurts so much it can be hard to breathe at times. Obsessive thoughts that do not take no for an answer are like bullies.

Although we all have emotional experiences, traumatized people can feel like they are at the mercy of their internal life. No one wants to have low self-esteem or be consumed by negativity and jealousy. Nor do we desire to be lonely and scared of life. These troubling states are not who we are: They are generated from the imprints of what happened to us. When we understand why we find ourselves stuck in negativity, we can more easily let go of shame and self-judgment.

Common mental and emotional consequences of childhood trauma are covered here.

Anger

Anger is a normal and healthy reaction to abuse and neglect. It is a response to injustice and powerlessness and the numbing agent for unbearable grief. Abused children are typically not able to protest mistreatment and often must suppress how they feel. It is simply not safe for them to speak up (fight) or leave an abusive situation (flight).

The price of suppressing years of childhood anger can be high. We are wired to complete our intended actions: to feel what we feel, say what we need to say, and do what we need to do. The consequences of holding it in can take a toll on our health. Suppressed anger activates a stress response in the body that impairs immune system functioning. Suppressed anger can also impact relationships. People who bully project anger meant for their abusers onto others. The same is true of drivers with road rage and people who make harsh comments on social media. Inappropriately expressed anger creates more pain for everyone involved. The saying "Hurt people hurt people" aptly and succinctly explains why. Anger is not wrong; the danger with it lies in its persistence and misdirected expression, as well as in using it to avoid dealing with our underlying pain.

Lindsey began therapy with me because she wanted to interact more positively with her son. She felt angry much of the time and didn't know why. As we explored her experiences growing up, it was clear that her parents were irritable and detached people who never expressed curiosity about her inner life and routinely invalidated and dismissed her needs. It never occurred to Lindsey that she experienced childhood trauma; in her mind, there were no major overt instances of abuse. Through our work, Lindsey realized her anger was related to the powerlessness and lack of nurturing she experienced throughout her childhood. She eventually saw how being intolerant of others was a symptom of unprocessed childhood anger.

Depression

Depression makes us unable to experience much if any pleasure in life. When we are depressed, we can feel powerless to change how we feel and often lack the motivation to do so. The benefit of depression is its invitation to go inward, to uncover the pain it has been protecting against.

Depression can present as chronic feelings of low mood or as debilitating feelings of emptiness and despair. Depression is essentially a calling for "deep rest." It is exhausting to experience chronic fear and unworthiness growing up and then go through adulthood unaware of the toll our difficult childhood is taking on us. It is hard to keep pushing through life as though nothing immensely wrong has happened.

Depression can result from learned helplessness or feeling completely unable to improve our situation. Kids who are systematically reminded their needs are inconsequential cope by convincing themselves it is best not to try. Depression often occurs as a result of feeling we must surrender our hopes and dreams. After years of feeling unseen, we may conclude our position in life is on the sidelines. When we are conditioned to believe we are incapable and undeserving of pursuing or achieving our desires, there is an emptiness inside that is hauntingly painful. When this happens, it is no wonder we find little pleasure and hope in life and succumb to the unbearable pain of depression.

Derrek's mother, an unstable woman who was unable to be nurturing to her children, left the family when Derrek was young. His dad was caring and well meaning but had his hands full as a single parent. Derrek was a quiet child who was careful not to be a burden and therefore felt invisible. He developed an avoidant attachment style because his emotional needs were persistently not met. As an adult, he was fearful of closeness with others but was also desperately lonely. The pain and emptiness he felt inside fueled his depression. Exploring and healing the original wounds that caused his difficulties helped Derrek make sense of his life and lessened his depression.

Resentment

Resentment is a form of anger. It is anger with a grudge. Some adults with developmental trauma experience denial about how poorly they were treated growing up. Their false perception of a close family leads to an inauthentic relationship with them. However, as the veil of denial lifts, resentment about how they were raised can emerge. After an EMDR session to address a complicated childhood, one client said, "I never realized what an asshole my mom was."

When we realize how much abuse we experienced in childhood, it is natural to feel resentment. This can be especially true when there has been no acknowledgment of wrongdoing. As a result of their pain, and the perspective that they should have been treated better, people with resentment can become critical, irritable, and stuck in self-pity. To move through the coldness of resentment, we must heal our original wounds and accept what we have been through. We must release the belief that life should have been a different way, which can often only happen as we find meaning in our suffering.

Anxiety

There are many presentations of anxiety. Anxiety can present as being worried, feeling unsettled, experiencing panic attacks, or being paralyzed with fear. Some people with anxiety shut down, whereas others become more talkative, irritable, or controlling. Some people can hide their anxiety, whereas others cannot, no matter how hard they try.

Anxiety can reflect the presence of stuck survival energy in the body because of nervous system activation in response to trauma. When we are propelled into a fight, flight, or freeze response, the survival energy generated to help us gets stuck if it is not released. This energy is then felt as sensation in our body, which people refer to as anxiety.

Anxiety is also the result of hypervigilance. Once trauma is experienced, whether it is birth trauma, medical trauma, or the result of abuse and neglect, we become hypervigilant, constantly on the lookout for danger, often perceiving nonthreats as threats. Unprocessed trauma generates the sense that something bad could happen at any time. For adults living with anxiety, everything can feel potentially dangerous. It's hard for adults with a trauma history to relax or accept that life is going more smoothly, because we are always "waiting for the other shoe to drop."

Shame

When we are not valued, it deeply impacts how we see ourselves. Not being properly loved and cared for not only leads to despair, fear, and powerlessness, but often makes us feel *responsible* for our own abuse. Young children lack the perspective to realize that mistreatment is a result of faulty parenting. Children believe that if they were somehow different, they would be treated better. This activates shame, not just for what they *did*, but for who they *are*. "I am bad," "I am not worthy," "I am not lovable," and "It is my fault" become many of the shame-filled beliefs of traumatized people.

Shame manifests in many ways. I see people who often unnecessarily apologize and presume they are a burden. One client said to me, "My apologizing is much better. I used to apologize to people who bumped into *me*." People also demonstrate shame-based behaviors, such as excessive regret and inability to forgive themselves for pain they unintentionally caused others.

Shannon began therapy after some difficult years with her teenage daughter. Their relationship had been tumultuous. Shannon felt she had failed her daughter but didn't understand why their relationship had been such a struggle. As we uncovered Shannon's story, it was clear she had a highly controlling father. She was expected to be perfect, and there were harsh consequences for mistakes. Even worse, Shannon was not allowed to cry. Before therapy she did not realize she had experienced childhood trauma, and she shamed herself for how she had punitively parented her children. In our work, Shannon faced the abuse from her childhood and acknowledged with her daughter how she had hurt her. As Shannon came to terms with her experiences as a child and as a mother, she was able to release her shame. Her relationship with her daughter was transformed, and they now enjoy a relationship based on mutual respect.

Guilt

Guilt can happen after a person says or does something that feels wrong. It can be productive guilt if it propels us to fix mistakes and change course. However, guilt can be unproductive when parents use it to manipulate their children. Many parents use guilt to coerce children into being "good." Parents may use phrases such as "I am so disappointed in you," "I can't believe you did that," and "Others have it worse." Being guilted by parents teaches us to put our own needs aside and comply to avoid being considered "bad."

Being put in caretaking roles by overwhelmed parents also creates a template for guilt. It conditions us to take care of others without thinking of our own needs. In these cases, self-sacrifice can become a dominant aspect of our identity, leading to guilt if we even consider putting our own needs first.

Guilt is also a consequence of being scapegoated. The scapegoated child carries the heavy burden of being the problem, the one responsible for hardship in the family. For example, Sara overheard her mother tell someone on the phone that she believed her daughter was the cause of her cancer. Even after her impressive dedication to being perfect to please her mother and avoid criticism, it still was not enough. This experience, combined with chronic criticism and blame, led to a lifelong pattern of Sara feeling unnecessarily guilty.

Sadness and Grief

Sadness and grief are emotional states emerging from loss. It is deeply saddening to grow up feeling unloved. We are wired for love and connection with our parents, and when it's missing, it is completely devastating. As we progress through life, feelings of loss accumulate. Developmental milestones, such as graduation, marriage, and having children, can be painful reminders of the absence of parents who care. Holidays, greeting cards, commercials, and social media posts portraying family togetherness can be a catalyst for depression, loneliness, and despair for those who desperately wish they had loving parents.

Jenna, a young adult woman who was falling in love, realized she did not want her boyfriend to meet her dad. In recent years, she had had very little contact with her father, who had narcissistically exerted control over her as a child, isolating her from others. Once she had someone special in her life, she began to recognize the depth of loss she was facing as the result of her childhood abuse, which included not having a father she could introduce her boyfriend to. The developmental stage of building a relationship with a partner activated a sense of grief that previously could not be accessed.

Negativity

It is unusual to encounter someone with significant unresolved trauma who presents as an optimist. Optimists are people who find it easy to see the good in life. They expect things to go well and easily see the silver linings in most situations. However, people dealing with extensive pain from childhood have been conditioned to view life negatively, as though difficulty and unpleasant outcomes are inevitable. After decades of hardship and disappointment, we believe "good things do not happen to me" and have ample evidence to verify this belief. We do not want to get our hopes up, only to again feel disappointed. To cope, we expect the worst. It may be more tolerable to be pleasantly surprised when good things happen than to be continually blindsided by life's disappointments. Adults who have a trauma-related pattern of negativity can complain a lot, see the worst in themselves and others, and have a hard time giving people the benefit of the doubt.

Low Self-Worth

As children, we formulate a sense of who we are based on how others interact with us. The body language, words, and actions of others form the mirror by which we interpret who we are. When we have the perception that the primary people in our lives are angry, disappointed, and annoyed with us, we believe we are deficient. We conclude that something is fundamentally wrong with us, which results in feelings of low self-worth.

Low self-worth makes it hard for us to confidently interact with the world. Social interactions create a host of potential land mines. Sydney, a mom of two, told me she chronically felt awkward around other parents. She often thought what she said was weird and wondered if other parents were judging her. Her insecurities made it hard to enjoy a mutual exchange with others. Wanting to be liked and accepted can be paralyzing for people with low self-worth.

Self-Doubt

It is important for children to feel a sense of personal power. When the people we are meant to trust validate our thoughts, opinions, and experiences, we develop confidence and learn to believe in ourselves. If adults do not help kids trust their internal knowing, kids learn to distrust their own gut. This creates a template of self-doubt that guides us to discount our perceptions.

Corrine described a sexual assault she experienced in elementary school. She told her parents what happened, but they downplayed the trauma and never spoke of it again. When her parents' reaction did not match her experience, she was terribly confused and doubted her own perception.

The nagging quality of self-doubt can be so chronic and familiar that many people do not even initially identify it as problematic. Self-doubt prevents people from fully engaging in life. Lack of confidence leads to inaction, keeping us from taking risks. We may not apply for a promotion, go on a date, attend a social function, or leave an abusive partner. We assume everyone else is more capable and likable than we are.

Judgment

Judgment is when a person determines someone or something is wrong, bad, or less than. This trait develops in childhood as a safety mechanism. When we are in potentially threatening situations, it's important to be able to properly judge the possibility of threats. This is one reason traumatized people can be especially judgmental. A dangerous childhood can finely tune this survival skill, which becomes overdeveloped and overused later in life.

Judgment is driven by insecurity. When we feel unsure, we numb and distract ourselves. We also project negative feelings onto others. For example, if we feel self-critical because of our weight, we might make fun of someone else we judge as being even more under- or overweight. A person who feels powerless may criticize others they deem weak. We identify faults in others as an attempt to feel better about our own limitations. Judgment is a temporary fix to soothe feelings of inadequacy.

Victim Mentality

As children we are at the mercy of those who care for us. When we are hurt growing up, we are victimized. Victimization generates feelings of powerlessness, hopelessness, and helplessness, leading to a victim mentality. Although we cannot bypass the pain generated from trauma, we also must not wallow in it. It is important to feel our feelings. We may yell, curse, scream, complain, and protest as we deal with the emotional upheaval associated with abandonment and betrayal. This is necessary for healing. Self-pity, however, can be seductive, especially if it invites attention and sympathy from others. This can lead to secondary gain, which essentially means that the attention people receive as a result of suffering inhibits them from getting better. The attention can seem as though it is filling a hole left from a lifetime of feeling invisible. Attention from others who feel sorry for us, though, does not help us heal.

Superiority

Superiority is the state of mind that convinces us we are better than someone else. It is the mental position that others, or certain people, are inferior to us in some manner. Although this may give the impression of confidence, the opposite is true: Confident people see themselves as equal to others, not superior. Adults with developmental trauma often feel deeply inadequate. By postulating exceptionality, we hope to garner the acceptance and admiration of others. We wanted these responses from our parents, and as a result can intensely seek validation by tooting our own horn.

Sometimes, superiority is presented as self-righteousness, which is the idea that one is a moral authority and therefore better than other people. I've known many adults who sought validation from religion in their quest to be considered "good" but experienced re-traumatization by the self-righteousness of leaders in religious settings who judged them as morally inadequate. People who consider themselves morally superior are often hiding from their own feelings of shame for behaviors they aren't ready to examine.

Lack of Trust

Vulnerability is terrifying for anyone who has been seriously hurt by another person. After abuse or neglect, we believe no one can be trusted. We assume people in positions of power will hurt us and partners will betray us. In contrast, some traumatized people do not trust others but struggle to set boundaries with trusting people who have not earned it.

We also often do not trust ourselves after abuse. Some part of us believes we could have prevented our mistreatment if only we had done something different or better. When we do not trust ourselves and others, it leads to immense internal conflict; it can feel like the only way to find relief is to control our external life as much as possible.

Seriousness

Kids are meant to laugh, create, express, and have fun. They are meant to feel carefree. Children are wired for curiosity and exploring. However, experiencing a lack of love and safety changes our orientation to life. Instead of living with innocence and lightheartedness, we become focused on self-protection, leading us to become serious people. Though some of us can have a good sense of humor and even choose comedy as a profession, laughter in many cases conceals deep-seated pain.

Self-Absorption

Many people who experience developmental trauma are raised by caregivers who do not consistently show interest in them. This is painful, confusing, and devastating for children who rely on parents for the development of self-worth. Children will cope by turning their attention inward, becoming excessively self-focused, or self-absorbed, to ensure that someone is paying attention to them. The consequence of this can be self-centeredness. We may talk extensively about ourselves while expressing little curiosity about others. We may quickly turn conversations back to ourselves, leaving others feeling as though they are an unnecessary participant in the interaction. Self-absorption is an attempt at feeling important and can be a beneficial coping strategy in childhood, but it is an alienating quality for adults.

Jealousy

When we are raised with lack, such as lack of love, friendship, shelter, and food, it is only natural to feel jealous of others who have these basic needs met. Adults often shame themselves for being jealous of others. However, I encourage people to allow feelings of jealousy to motivate them. It can be valuable to identify the desires unearthed by jealousy. Desire helps mobilize efforts to meet our needs.

Growing up I frequently felt jealous of others who had attentive parents. I observed that some of my friends were treated respectfully by their parents, and I longed for the same kind of treatment. This jealousy served a valuable purpose for me. It fueled my determination to treat my own kids with the respect and attention that I missed out on.

These descriptions of common mental and emotional consequences of childhood trauma are meant to help you become more aware of the impact of childhood trauma on how you think and feel in your adult life. These patterns reflect your best efforts to cope and manage unhealed pain. We cannot grow up in complex and painful circumstances without it deeply impacting how we operate in life. Offer yourself compassion for the fact that the trauma you experienced growing up necessitated the emergence of these painful patterns. These traits do not have to be permanent attributes.

There are many ways to heal. You can begin by taking note of the mental and emotional patterns with which you identify. Then you can become more mindful in your day-to-day life when you find yourself being judgmental, being overly serious, or feeling guilty. Healing our original trauma will slowly reduce these trauma side effects, but awareness of your mental and emotional patterns can help you begin to break the addictive responses of unconsciously acting out your trauma narrative.

Chapter 10

Self-Abuse

Behaviors are cues containing information about a person's internal life. Eating is a behavior resulting from the internal feelings of hunger—or the pattern of numbing to suppress emotional discomfort. Yelling is a behavior that comes from anger—or fear. Squealing with delight is a behavior related to joy. Self-abuse involves a host of behaviors that reflect difficulty with emotion regulation and an internal need to punish ourselves—or to try to feel alive. Self-abuse occurs in a variety of ways and can feel so normal that many people don't even know they are doing it. In truth, our behavior always has a story to tell.

When we have been hurt as children, our behavior reflects mistrust of others and the expectation of harm. It can also mirror the disdain we feel toward ourselves, which matches how our parents treated us. Any behaviors that are not a reflection of love, whether toward others or ourselves, are indicators of trauma and signs that we are disconnected from Essence.

This chapter will help you identify your patterns related to self-abuse. Without awareness, we blindly hurt ourselves. When we can instead recognize how childhood trauma reflects how we treat ourselves, we create a greater possibility of transformation.

Self-Injury

Self-injury is an attempt to cope with unbearable pain. When we cut, burn, or injure ourselves in other ways, an endorphin rush follows. This can make self-harm feel pleasurable. For people who have few other ways to feel good, cutting can be enticing because of the relief it brings. We also self-harm to bring us back into our bodies. When we dissociate and feel depersonalized, or feel we are outside of our own body, the presence of pain, blood, and bruising can make us feel real and alive.

We can also hurt ourselves as a form of self-punishment. We may misperceive our body as the enemy or think our body could have done more to protect us, particularly when there has been sexual abuse. We may feel excessive shame for what we have or haven't done and for other self-judgments, including that we are flawed, unworthy, or somehow deficient. We may have eating disorders and misuse laxatives, induce vomiting, restrict food, and exercise excessively.

In all cases, self-injury is an attempt to feel better. Dr. Pat Ogden, creator of sensorimotor psychotherapy, says every symptom is a survival response. To address this trauma symptom, and all trauma symptoms, it is important to understand the purpose of the behavior and the underlying beliefs and trauma experiences that created it.

Addiction

Addiction is a self-abuse coping strategy stemming from difficulty with emotion regulation and lack of love. Dr. Gabor Maté explains that addictions function as an attempt to fill the emptiness created by attachment wounds. Because of a damaged attachment relationship with a caregiver, our brain circuits do not develop properly, leaving us with deep emotional pain and few, if any, tools for providing relief. When we feel unbearable emotional pain and have no helpful strategies for coping, desperation sets in. Desperation can lead to detrimental behaviors. When addictions bring relief, the benefits can feel worth the cost, at least at the time.

When a person uses sex, drugs, shopping, exercise, or workaholism to suppress pain, changes in the brain elicit the chemical composition mimicking the feeling of love. In his TED Talk, Dr. Maté said his patients explained that when they were high, they felt normal and free of pain. To someone who felt unloved growing up, the boost of endorphins, dopamine, and oxytocin (the love hormone) that accompanies drug use is seductive. In fact, for people in extreme emotional pain, addiction can take precedence over anything else in life, including their home, job, and family.

Self-Sabotage

Showing up late to a coveted job interview, misplacing a paycheck, and eating an entire container of ice cream when we have a dairy allergy are all examples of self-sabotage. Self-sabotage is any behavior that prevents us from achieving freedom, fun, peace, happiness, vitality, and personal fulfillment. These unwanted but sneaky and persistent happiness-preventing behaviors are the result of a protective mechanism designed to keep us small and safe.

When our brain has been wired to expect danger, it wants us to change very little. The hypervigilance serving as a high-powered and well-trained security officer is convinced that when we vary our life too much, we are at risk for danger.

Change involves the unknown, and our brain wants to keep life predictable so it can more effectively protect us.

The internal working model plays a large role in self-sabotage, with beliefs such as "I am not worthy," "I am a failure," "Life is hard," and "Dreams come true only for others." Our beliefs largely determine what we experience in life. Therefore, if we have a desire to pursue an exciting new job but our beliefs are aligned with failure, we are unlikely to fully achieve what we desire professionally. If we long for financial freedom but believe we are stuck living paycheck to paycheck, we can sabotage our ability to have financial abundance.

Approval Seeking

Validation is one of the most important responses a child can receive from a caregiver. As children we need to know that our thoughts, feelings, and reactions are acceptable. Attention, affection, connection, validation, and approval are the nourishment children need to feel safe and worthy. Being raised by wounded parents severely limits the possibility of getting the attention and validation children need. When children are not validated, the desire for approval never goes away. In fact, the lack of approval from parents can lead to an insatiable craving for validation.

In many cases, whatever we are seeking from others is an indicator of what we need to give ourselves. When I sought comfort for chronic pain, it was often an indicator I needed more self-compassion. This did not mean that I shouldn't have asked for comfort, but that I was missing the point if I was seeking comfort only from outside myself. Pain and other symptoms can be an invitation from the body to bring more loving presence to ourselves. The excessive desire to be seen by others can be a sign we are neglecting ourselves. When we become adults, the only approval we need is our own.

Complex Relationship with Food

Many people with developmental trauma experience suffering around food. Food is a metaphor for nurturing. Wounded parents with distorted views of love typically do not feed their children properly. Some children are fed little, either because of poverty or as a means of parental control. Some children are abusively forced to eat everything on their plate. Others are sadistically made to watch their parents eat while they are deprived of food. Some wounded children have a desire to be invisible and therefore eat very little, and others want to be protected from sexual abuse, so they eat excessively to gain weight as a defense against it. Others learn to suppress their desire for food because it is painful to need something that is scarce.

In adult life, food issues surface in a variety of ways. We may justify overeating because of our history of being deprived or control our bodies by exercising extreme discipline with food. Many traumatized people place little value on the quality of their food. Processed food, sugary drinks, excessive caffeine, and foods laced with pesticides are common food choices for people who undervalue themselves. We can either harm ourselves with food or love ourselves with food. Cycle breakers aspire to choose love.

Consider which of the above self-abuse behavior patterns you use to cope with the impact of childhood trauma. Hold yourself with kindness as you do this. A difficult childhood always has a considerable impact on adult life. The presence of these patterns is not an indicator of weakness or failure; it is an indicator of pain.

Chapter 11

Relationship Consequences

Both intimate and social relationships can be problematic for people with developmental trauma. Some consequences of childhood abuse arise only when interacting with others because trauma was a relational problem in childhood, creating the template that relationships are threatening. Childhood may have taught us that relationships are the source of being used, ignored, scapegoated, gaslit, and physically and sexually harmed. These trauma imprints are often at the heart of misunderstandings, tension, and conflict with others. We want to be loved, so we may find we are equally drawn to and repelled by connection with others.

When we have challenges with people, including partners, children, friends, and coworkers, we can find that problems reflect specific relationship patterns we experienced growing up. After feeling abandoned, we may avoid closeness to prevent being hurt. Witnessing our mother dominate our father may be reflected in our tendency to be controlled in a relationship or to control others. Being harshly punished if we did not do our chores correctly may make us hypercritical about how family members should handle household tasks. We often repeat what we know.

Relationship problems are associated with limiting beliefs. If we believe we aren't capable of love, we may find ourselves single or in destructive relationships. If we believe men or women are undependable, we may see only how partners disappoint us or pick a partner who is unreliable. Behaving in an entitled manner in relationships can result from the belief that others exist to serve us.

Improper expectations can also contaminate relationships. Wounded adults may believe that partners or others will correct their parents' mistakes. If parents did not pay attention to us, we may overly demand attention from partners. If parents were critical, we may expect that partners will excessively admire and praise us. It is important to identify what's at the heart of problematic interactions with others, whether they are our child, partner, friend, coworker, or even a waiter or salesperson. Uncovering hidden expectations can help resolve relationship struggles and show us what needs healing.

Common trauma-based patterns in relationships are discussed here.

Isolation

Many adults with developmental trauma prefer to keep to themselves. They may have underdeveloped social relationships because they don't trust in others and have low self-esteem. People who have a pattern of self-isolation can be guided by beliefs such as "I can't depend on others," "The world is an unpredictable place," and "Other people take advantage of me." As one woman put it, "I would rather hang out with my dogs. They are more loyal than people." As a result, social encounters can be limited and superficial, and we may go to great lengths to avoid relationships because deep connections require vulnerability.

Our wiring for connection complicates the tendency to self-isolate. Many traumatized adults both fear and deeply crave meaningful relationships. This creates an internal struggle, a vacillation between avoiding social interactions while feeling lonely and engaging socially but suffering from anxiety. Unless the underlying experiences and beliefs related to low self-worth and distrust are healed, isolation and loneliness can persist.

Blaming Others

For some, trauma begins in infancy, when dependent babies have no ability to protect themselves from troubled parents who hurt them. To recover, children need parents to repair their mistakes. When that doesn't happen, a relationship imprint occurs, convincing us that people who hurt us do not take accountability. The ensuing belief can become "I am wounded and it's your fault." This template can fuel an intense need for someone to acknowledge wrongdoing. When we are not conscious of this belief, we can unfairly blame others because of the suppressed anger toward our parents for their lack of accountability.

Adults can also have a pattern of blaming others if they were shamed and demoralized by parents when they made a mistake. When this happens, humiliation is wired together with fault, so we do whatever it takes to avoid accountability and therefore avoid further humiliation. The belief template related to blame can be "It's my fault and I am bad."

When we are determined to break intergenerational cycles of abuse, we commit to taking responsibility for our life, which requires us to stop blaming others. This means we make reparations when we are wrong, and we hold ourselves accountable for healing our original traumas. We therefore take responsibility for our lives instead of feeling limited by others' behavior.

Shelley initiated therapy because she felt burdened by her partner's reliance on her to fix problems. Her partner lacked assertiveness and struggled to find fulfillment in life. Shelley wanted to help but also resented her partner's helplessness and blamed her for the relationship dynamic. As we explored this relationship pattern, Shelley realized her mother relied on her father to meet all her needs. When Shelley recognized she was replicating the over-functioner / under-functioner dynamic she witnessed growing up, she was able to take more responsibility for addressing her part in the relationship troubles.

Need to Control

Healthy relationships have a foundation of trust. Because the internal working models of traumatized adults guide them to distrust themselves, the world, and others, all relationships can be difficult. These adults may seek to control wherever they can to compensate for feeling powerless. Controlling behavior is an attempt to reduce anxiety by trying to prevent powerlessness. The belief template of those who need to control others is "I am not safe."

Distrust makes it hard to give another person the benefit of the doubt, which is an important dynamic in successful relationships. Distrust can lead to jealousy and suspicion, causing us to behave insecurely. A distrusting partner may suspect his wife is having an affair despite no concrete evidence. An exchange between a receptionist and a customer can become tense when the traumatized person assumes he was intentionally mistreated.

The need to control can emerge in various ways. At a dinner party, the hostess handed me a loaf of bread to cut, giving me explicit and extensive details on precisely how to do it rather than trusting this simple task could be done in a satisfactory manner. A more extreme version of the need to control is abusive behavior, when the traumatized person limits a partner's contact with others and makes unreasonable demands. Other examples include giving frequent, unsolicited advice, demanding that we have our own way, and anxiously needing an immaculate home.

Codependency

To some degree, we are dependent beings. We're designed to rely on others. In a healthy relationship, we feel safe to clearly express our needs and there is no need to manipulate our partner to give us space, pick up dinner, or express affection. However, wounded people who were conditioned in childhood to suppress needs have a hard time asking directly for what they need or want. This pattern can begin in infancy when parents do not properly respond to them when they cry and continues in the various ways parents convey to children that their needs do not matter. We are conditioned to deny that we have needs because of our fear of rejection. The beliefs associated with this form of trauma can be "It's not safe to ask for my needs to be met" and "I am responsible for the well-being of others."

Adults with a history of rejection can become triggered when they need support and connection because they do not feel safe asking for it. In these cases, we create indirect ways to have our needs met, which leads to codependency, a dependence on another person to feel good. This may mean we feel responsible for the happiness, well-being, and behavior of others, or we believe others are responsible for making us happy.

The following are common indicators that a person is engaged in codependent behavior:

- Need for approval, acceptance, and validation from others
- Inability to leave an abusive relationship
- Making excuses for the misbehavior of others
- Need to control others
- Difficulty asserting oneself in relationships
- Belief that a person must save another person from bad decisions

Jason began therapy to address long-standing feelings of anger. Part of our time was spent addressing parenting matters regarding his adult sons. They meant the world to him. He had been determined to raise responsible children who had no regrets. We discussed how he routinely advised his adult sons about jobs, relationships, living arrangements, and other things. I pointed out how his relationship with his children was codependent, and we explored the fears underneath his well-meaning but controlling behavior.

Jason realized that being intrusive with his sons was related to watching his brother make many mistakes that led to addiction, prison, and not contributing meaningfully to society. As a result, Jason parented out of fear; he used defensive parenting by trying to prevent his children from making mistakes instead of teaching them to make decisions for themselves. With this new understanding about his codependent behavior, Jason began practicing staying in his own lane while also doing the deep healing work associated with abuse from childhood. The result has been much more satisfying relationships with his boys.

Poor Boundaries

As children we learn boundaries by watching how others set them and observing the outcome. When children witness domestic violence, they witness a violation of boundaries. When children are abused, they experience a violation of boundaries. These situations lay the foundation for what they expect with regard to boundaries in future relationships. When parents violate boundaries, children are essentially taught "You do not have the right to say no," "You are incapable of saying no," and "It does not matter if you say no." Children carry these distorted perceptions of boundaries into adulthood. Boundary setting can be a foreign concept for people who grew up learning that what they wanted did not matter. As one client said, "I didn't even realize boundaries were a thing."

Tolerating Bad Behavior

Being traumatized can give us a high tolerance for emotional pain. This tolerance for pain can feel so normal, it may not occur to us that boundaries need to be set.

A sense of being powerless and defenseless can cause people with developmental trauma to not even notice or be alarmed when they are mistreated. Even if they do notice, they may not realize they have a choice. Personal agency is the capacity to influence our own life. This is often seriously limited for people who were not allowed to set limits for themselves.

Julia described multiple narcissistic boyfriends she had as a teenager. Each time, she was lured into these relationships with the promise of love that quickly turned to control. Her hunger for connection made it difficult to see past the facade of love. A secure child would have seen the red flags and not tolerated being treated badly. In Julia's case, the pattern was so familiar, she could not discern the differences between a partner who cared about her and one who was using her.

The inner turmoil people with developmental trauma experience impacts adult relationships in a variety of ways. To break the cycle of problematic relationships, you must identify your trauma-driven behaviors so you stop operating on autopilot. First comes insight and awareness. Next is trauma work to clear limiting beliefs and heal your wounds. Then prepare yourself for fulfillment in relationships you may have never thought possible.

Chapter 12

Suicidal Ideation

In graduate school I volunteered as a teaching assistant for a popular teacher who taught an undergraduate class on death and dying. I asked her why she thought people died by suicide. She said, "Tunnel vision." When people feel hopeless, she explained, they believe there is no possibility that their life circumstances will change, and they cannot bear to live the rest of their life as it is.

The ability to regulate our emotional state is a cornerstone of well-being. However, for those of us with fear, shame, and a constant expectation of doom, being able to lift ourselves out of a dark place can be extraordinarily difficult. Working through difficulties and building resiliency helps strengthen our ability to cope and heal. But no matter how much resiliency a person has cultivated, despair can feel overpowering at times.

The level of anguish and hopelessness that leads a person to suicidal thinking is heartbreaking. Our society lacks understanding about suicidal ideation, and often assumes suicidal thinking is selfish or that those who make suicide attempts are merely seeking attention. These limiting views on suicide are stunningly absent of compassion. As a result, people are often ashamed for making suicide attempts and feel they should apologize. However, people who are suicidal are in pain.

Trauma symptoms often separate us from others, putting us at risk for suicidal thinking. Traumatized people can feel that no one can understand the depth of their pain, even if they try. To describe what this was like, one woman told me, "Everyone else is on Earth, and I am on Pluto." These people may isolate themselves because of anxiety, lack of trust, or health issues. They may be rejected because of self-centeredness, problems with anger, or social awkwardness. I've heard some people with suicidal ideation say they feel so insignificant to others that they don't think anyone would even notice or care if they were gone. People in a lot of pain are at a high risk of giving up on life. They do not necessarily want to die, but they want their suffering to end. After numerous unsuccessful attempts to curb their pain, suicide may feel like the only option.

Paramount to thriving after trauma is the ability to make meaning of atrocity. Suicide prevention relies on our capacity to soul search, to uncover both the reasons and the solutions for our suffering. When we are disconnected from Essence, our reverence for life is limited. The existential crisis embedded in deeply painful traumatic experiences naturally limits our awareness of the Divine. Connection to Divinity can provide strength to weather tough times, and its absence can lead to despair. Pulling ourselves out of the agony of despair requires the kind of strength that can be hard for non-suicidal people to understand.

One milestone of trauma healing is recognizing that life is worth living, no matter how we feel. It can be tricky for people who are in the early stages of recovery from developmental trauma to convince themselves of this. They may feel incapable of cultivating happiness or feel so fundamentally flawed that a meaningful life seems completely out of reach. They may believe that it is impossible to change their life circumstances. However, this stance is based on their trauma history and is maintained by their internal working model. Trauma-based beliefs such as "Life will never get better," "Life is meaningless," and "I will never be happy" developed when life felt hopeless. Although these people may have been powerless in childhood, they have autonomy as adults. Beliefs can change and trauma can be healed.

One client told me that before beginning therapy she prayed every night to God that she would die in her sleep. She felt miserable and had no hope that she could ever feel good or have a meaningful life. After a few months of therapy she said, "I would be so disappointed if I died now. There is so much I want to do." I believe we are all capable of this turnaround.

A personal note here for anyone contemplating suicide. Please consider that even though you may be facing what feels like insurmountable pain, there is a remarkable amount of possibility for you. What you feel now can be temporary. Please know that this can pass. You can move through your pain and create a highly meaningful and joyful life, no matter what you have been through, how you feel now, and the current state of your life. It is your birthright to have a good life, and there is a path to it for you. You can think about it like this quote shared with me by a client: "Everything will be all right in the end. If it is not all right, it's not the end."

Chapter 13

Physical Consequences

When we are exposed as young children to experiences that do not support healthy development, there are deep imprints in our physiology. The priority of the physical body changes from being relaxed to preparing for danger. Hypervigilance becomes our default mode, leading to physical consequences, including muscle tension, hormonal imbalances, difficulty focusing, pain, poor digestion, autoimmune issues, and adrenal fatigue. Top trauma experts such as Dr. Gabor Maté and Dr. Bessel van der Kolk agree that the constant stress with which scared children live takes an enormous toll on the physical body and is a primary cause of most chronic illness.

If someone has a chronic health condition such as Crohn's disease, fibromyalgia, irritable bowel syndrome, or Hashimoto's thyroiditis, they very likely grew up with developmental trauma or experienced high levels of stress for another reason. I came to this realization after suffering with a variety of chronic health issues for more than thirty years.

Around age eighteen I began having intense pelvic pain. I had no idea why and had no success resolving it. After the birth of my first daughter I had an additional health challenge and did not fully recover. My second daughter was born less than two years later, and my health declined further. I was exhausted, and though my physician indicated my postpartum thyroid issue was resolved after a few months, there was clearly something wrong.

Despite never feeling well, I pushed myself to be the best therapist, wife, and mother I could be. As a perfectionist, I wanted to shine in all areas of my life. However, I was plagued with disabling fatigue, chronic pain, anxiety, and depression. I had many unexplained health symptoms, including burning in my hands and feet, migraines, nerve and muscle pain, sensitivity to chemicals, bladder issues, digestive problems, burning mouth syndrome, and pelvic pain. I was also hypersensitive to lights, sounds, smells, and touch. Additionally, I had a bout with viral meningitis and a heart condition called ventricular tachycardia.

In a desperate effort to improve my health, I met with many physicians who were consistently puzzled by my complex symptoms. The immense difficulty caused by living with such physical discomfort was made worse by routine shaming from doctors, which seemed to stem from their inability to help me. I eventually left conventional medicine to find answers through holistic care. With alternative medicine, some of my symptoms improved, but my overall health was not good.

A few years later, my massage therapist, Susan, suggested I have a sleep study. I told her I thought I slept fine, even though I was always exhausted, but I took her advice anyway. The results of my sleep study pointed out I was unknowingly waking up nearly 180 times a night, and I received multiple sleep disorder diagnoses, including narcolepsy. I felt I finally had an explanation for my constant exhaustion. I began medication that forced me into a very deep sleep each night. However, my health continued to deteriorate.

Two years later, I had heart palpitations for the second time. I was weak and fatigued, and my brain was not functioning well. One day while my preteen daughter was home sick I called and asked if she needed me to get anything for her. She requested bagels. To my alarm, I felt totally confused about how to find the bagel shop I had been to many times, despite the fact it was on the same street as the physical therapy office I had just left.

Soon after this, my health made it impossible to work. I had no idea what was wrong with me, despite years of seeking both conventional and holistic help.

I did not know it at the time but hitting rock bottom was an important catalyst for the journey leading to the recovery of my physical health and a spiritual awakening leading to the recovery of my authentic self. My overwhelming, long-standing health crisis was the gateway to creating a vibrant and happy life.

Like so many people who grew up with developmental trauma, I had no idea how traumatized I was, which seriously limited my ability to connect my poor health to what I experienced in childhood. My coping mechanisms allowed me to navigate important facets of life like finding a good life partner, getting graduate degrees, having children, and running a small business. However, beneath the massive protection I masterfully developed were deep feelings of inadequacy and extreme fear. Out of service to me, my body stored emotional pain from childhood so I could manage a difficult life. However, after many years of this, my body had reached its limit.

The Trauma Response Cycle

For people with developmental trauma, excessive activation of the trauma response cycle is a factor contributing to chronic health conditions. This is the reaction we experience when under threat of harm. This in and of itself is not harmful. The problem is the frequency with which this response is necessary for children who do not feel safe.

Early in every trauma response is a behavior called *orienting* in which a person scans the environment for danger if a threat is suspected. Once danger is detected, a defense strategy is selected. There are four options for responding when anyone feels threatened. First, we can *fight* to defend ourselves, from physically fighting off an attacker to verbally asserting "get away from me" or "leave me alone." A second healthy reaction to emotional or physical danger is *flight*, meaning a person physically leaves a threatening situation. A third alternative is *social engagement*, reaching out to someone who can effectively provide aid, whether it is a known person, a stranger, or even the person causing the harm (known as fawning).

When one of these three strategies works, we bring resolution to the trauma response and can feel elated about successfully averting harm. The survival energy activated when the threat was detected gets discharged and we can return to baseline functioning. However, when none of these three strategies are possible, which is typically the case for children who are helpless at the hands of hurtful caregivers, the body automatically engages the *freeze* response. This response entails bracing for protection and then collapsing or becoming immobile.

Everyone can relate to having activated threat responses. We have all experienced frightening situations, from terrifying life-threatening events such as a car accident, sexual assault, or physical assault to getting cut off in traffic, being belittled by a boss, or being physically injured. Trauma responses are essential. In the face of real danger, it is critical to respond in a way that ensures survival. When survival responses successfully help us escape danger, the stress from the event can be more easily discharged, which helps prevent post-traumatic stress disorder (PTSD).

When a person lives in a threatening environment, trauma responses do not turn off. This demands a high state of alert, which necessitates constant engagement of the sympathetic nervous system, leading to a continual state of fight-or-flight-or-freeze. In these cases, stress hormones such as adrenaline and cortisol constantly course through our body. Although the trauma response cycle is intended to prepare a child to manage danger, there is a high price to pay when it is routinely activated. One cost is chronic illness.

In his book *When the Body Says No,* Dr. Gabor Maté explains how chronic stress leads to chronic illness:

> Emotions influence—and are influenced by—the functioning of our major organs, the integrity of our immune defences and the workings of the many circulating biological substances that help govern the body's states. When emotions are repressed . . . this inhibition disarms the body's defences against illness. Repression, dissociating emotions from awareness and relegating them to the unconscious realm—disorganizes and confuses our physiological defences so that in some people these defenses go awry, becoming the destroyers of health rather than its protectors. (p. 7)

In his book *The Body Keeps the Score,* Bessel van der Kolk also addresses the relationship between chronic stress and illness:

> When people are chronically angry or scared, constant muscle tension ultimately leads to spasms, back pain, migraine headaches, fibromyalgia, and other forms of chronic pain. They may visit multiple specialists, undergo extensive diagnostic tests, and be prescribed multiple medications, some of which may provide temporary relief but all of which fail to address the underlying issues. (p. 268)

Maybe you have a complex health profile like me. Or perhaps you have minor digestive issues, difficulty concentrating, lower back pain, acid reflux, insomnia, joint pain, or tinnitus. Maybe you've been told you will be on medication the rest of your life or surgery is your only option. I'm not at liberty to offer medical advice here, nor should I. However, what I can tell you is that when people are determined to heal, regardless of the condition, progress is possible, if not complete resolution. One of the best things a doctor said to me many years ago about the cocktail of medication I was taking is that I would likely be taking it the rest of my life. That's the perfect thing to tell a stubborn person. It was precisely the fuel I needed to say to myself, *Watch me*. I am now medication-free and have been for a long time.

The connection between childhood trauma and chronic illness has not yet achieved major mainstream awareness, but I am optimistic our society will become more informed about trauma in time. I have found that holistically trained providers are more likely to understand the connection between poor health and chronic nervous system activation. If you are dealing with chronic health challenges, I encourage you to carefully select practitioners who treat the whole person and are skilled at addressing the root cause of illness.

Part III
EMPOWERMENT

Tasks of Recovering from Childhood Trauma

Healing from childhood trauma is a journey of discovering who we really are. It is the process of releasing the negative emotions, perceptions, and beliefs developed during our formative years that are not in alignment with the truth of our authentic self. Healing requires the body to let go of defensive protective postures and fear. It involves healing our inner child and learning to love. We let go of the past and learn to live in the now. The process of healing restores our authenticity. The result is wholeness, or reconnection with our Essence. We heal ourselves by becoming empowered, thereby letting go of victimhood.

Society has the mistaken perception that one person can rescue another, and it has many avenues for unconsciously reinforcing disempowerment. The music industry illustrates our society's addiction to codependency with songs about controlling, revenge, and fixing. Dating reality shows depict young men and women who are convinced another person can make them happy. It is seductive to give our power to others because of our desperate and unconscious desire to be taken care of, a desire that stems from childhood neglect. However, a life we love has very little room for self-pity and overdependence on others. Wellness requires us to surrender the expectation that anyone can rescue or complete us.

Empowerment includes putting ourselves first, setting boundaries, and releasing the need to impress, please, and win the approval of others. It is taking full responsibility for our life, being our own hero, warrior, best friend, confidant, and cheerleader. Additionally, empowerment is being kind and gentle with ourselves when we cannot do any of the above.

Part III covers the 16 Pillars of Trauma Recovery. These pillars contain information designed to guide and support your return to wholeness. These pillars are interconnected like a web, none of them standing alone. The common element is empowerment: Each pillar assumes you are willing to live an empowered life by facing the tasks necessary to heal. Healing is courageous. It is hard work. Though it can take considerable effort to transcend a life of pain, you can create a life you love, even though your life may currently be very challenging. It begins with an acknowledgment that the responsibility of healing is yours alone.

Once you say yes to your healing journey, the path will be laid out before you in Divine timing. You will not be given the whole map, just the information you need for the present step. Synchronistic occurrences will appear, assuring that you are on the right path. Synchronicities include seeing repeating numbers, hearing the same message from multiple sources, and other fun, indisputable messages confirming that you are guided and supported.

For example, I have a friend who was raised to be religious. As her spiritual views evolved, she developed a healing business that her religious peers did not approve of. She felt conflicted. She loved her work but questioned if, indeed, she was professionally out of alignment with her religious upbringing. In her quest for truth, she made a declaration to God: "I love my work and want to continue what I am doing, but I just want to know I am not doing someone wrong. Let me know. Make it obvious. Treat me like I am dumb and spell it out in black and white." A short time later, she was getting a Reiki massage. During the massage, the therapist paused and wrote something on a piece of paper. She told my friend she didn't know what the message meant but said she felt it was intended for her. On the paper were the words, spelled out in black and white: "You are not doing anything wrong." This message of verification helped my friend move confidently forward in her spiritual work.

I once listened to a motivational speech about how to become a millionaire. The speaker said the value of creating wealth is *who* we must become to achieve the abundance we desire. He was referring to the importance of cultivating qualities such as vision, determination, confidence, courage, and discipline. Essentially, wealth then becomes a by-product of the well-being we cultivate, which is the true source of our abundance. The same idea is true for people recovering from developmental trauma. As we reconnect with our Essence by healing our trauma and resurrecting our authenticity, everything we desire can fall into place.

As you do what it takes to heal, you return to who you really are and more naturally embody the qualities of strength, love, compassion, patience, and contentment. The 16 Pillars of Trauma Recovery are presented as a guide to encourage you to reclaim your power and create the wonderful life you have always wanted.

Personal Responsibility

M any wounded people dealing with the complexities of being traumatized can be burdened with the question "Why me?" We can feel robbed of a happy childhood. We may wish we had not been harmed, had had better parents, and had received the support, validation, kindness, and acknowledgment we wanted and needed. This question can inform our perception that the partner who left us, the teacher who didn't like us, and even the fact that our car keeps breaking down are signs that the universe is against us.

At some point, everyone with childhood trauma feels a sense of victimization, because we were victimized. To create a meaningful and fulfilling life, however, we need to find a way to acknowledge and heal our pain and let go of our impossible wishes for what wasn't and what cannot be. We stay victimized when we are unable to let go of the fact we were hurt as children by our parents or by others.

We come to Earth with a plan. Each of us has a distinct purpose, a specific way we are meant to contribute to the evolution of humanity. Before our incarnation, our soul knows the life experiences we need for our growth that could make it possible to fulfill our purpose. Our childhood experiences, including loss, abuse, and other hardships, as well as positive experiences such as a meaningful teacher, best friend, special pet, or a trip to the ocean for a future marine biologist, are all designed with the purpose of preparing us for our life mission. When we accept that we chose our life, we gain freedom.

Robert Schwartz, author of *Your Soul's Gift: The Healing Power of the Life You Planned Before You Were Born*, is a hypnotherapist. He provides between-life regressions for clients who want to learn about their pre-birth planning session to know what their soul planned for this life and why. He wrote that he personally experienced severe emotional abuse from his mother, the purpose of which he said was to "foster his evolution." If one of our life lessons is overcoming helplessness, we can be born into families who take our power. If we are to learn forgiveness, we need people in our lives who are difficult to forgive. Before we incarnate, we make agreements with others—with parents, siblings, pets, partners, children, and others—about the role we will play in each other's growth. All these agreements are made to evolve our soul. This knowledge can help remove a sense of victimization regarding a difficult childhood.

Adults with a history of developmental trauma who feel stuck often feel entitled to have had a better life. They can't move past the position of "It's not fair" or "It shouldn't have happened." Being a cycle breaker, though, demands a willingness to move beyond the perception of victim. I know this can be tough; I embraced victimhood for a long time. I still sometimes feel sorry for myself. I understand the enticement of self-pity, which is a distraction from grief, anger, disappointment, and despair. However, if you are ready to step out of the notion of victimization, you must accept ownership for your life and everything in it. The means to empowerment is personal responsibility, which motivates us to take our life into our own hands instead of waiting for a rescue or an apology that will never materialize.

We can learn from Viktor Frankl, author of *Man's Search for Meaning*, who survived the Holocaust by finding meaning in the experience. He said, "Everything can be taken from a man but one thing: the last of the human freedoms—to choose one's attitude in any given set of circumstances, to choose one's own way" (p. 66). He taught that our ability to respond to adversity and take responsibility for our lives is the predominant means of finding fulfillment in life.

Taking personal responsibility for our lives involves accepting that everything is in Divine order and that we are the captain of our own ship. We do not wait for anyone else to make things better for us. *We* make things better for us.

Though for many years I longed for my parents to acknowledge how they hurt me and to be the parents I wanted, I ultimately concluded these wishes were futile. I realized my parents were just playing assigned roles in their relationship with me, following the agreement made before we incarnated. On a human level, my staying in contact with my parents was destructive for me, and it was necessary for me to cut off contact with them. On a spiritual level, all was as it should be. There are times when I wish they hadn't played their parts so well, of course, but taking personal responsibility for my life has enabled me to heal and embrace my mission, which is to assist traumatized people in returning to wholeness. The depth of suffering I experienced has afforded me the capacity to easily hold space for others with devastating pain. This capability has been possible only because of what I have been through and overcome.

It is our decision what we do with our pain. Staying stuck and angry is a choice. This choice may be temporary, or it may be permanent. Cycle breakers ultimately decide to use difficult life experiences as fuel for transformation. As we heal, we transform hardship into ease, hate into love, people pleasing into boundary setting, and agony into joy. If you are reading this book, you are seeking transcendence of suffering. Start by taking responsibility for your life where you can. Work to be more mindful of times when you blame someone else for your pain, when you feel bitter about the injustice in your life, and when you hold others responsible for how you are doing. Decide if you want to stay angry or if you want to create a life you love. If you are not ready to move forward at this point, it's okay. You can always choose again.

Pillar 2

Embrace Difficulties

An aspiration for spiritual people is to be in the flow, where there is an abundance of ease and success. The flow is an indicator of connection to Essence. I've told my competitive daughter that we are either winning or we are learning. Being the victor in competition feels good, but the sting of defeat can reveal the chinks in our armor that need to be repaired. What feels like a loss can be a forthcoming triumph in disguise. A good loss can fuel a bigger win when the time is right, if we properly parlay the wisdom accessible to us from the setback. This is true whether the perceived loss is in a competition, a challenge with a coworker, or dealing with illness and chronic pain.

Victory and ease rely on our belief system. When we believe life is fun, it is. When we believe we are worthy of landing the lead role in a play, we can. When we believe we are financially abundant, money can appear in delightful and unexpected ways. To create a life of ease, we must release limiting beliefs related to the expectations of hardship and transform our trauma. The purpose of difficulty is to reveal to us what needs to be healed, to show us how strong we are, and to give us opportunities to further develop characteristics needed for our purpose. Challenge equals growth potential. Accepting difficulties as beneficial can soften our resistance when we encounter unwanted hardships.

I've heard it said there will never be a cure for the common cold because of the service it provides us. Colds give us a reason to rest when we have overdone it and give our immune system an opportunity to stay in shape. Even though cold symptoms are unpleasant, they can be necessary for our well-being. Healing from developmental trauma requires us to navigate a variety of challenges, which, like being sick, can be unpleasant but still in service of our highest good. Challenges test and increase our internal strength, aiding in the cultivation of qualities such as patience, self-confidence, compassion, persistence, and trust.

In many significant holy books, we are guided to "look the devil in the eye." This means it is best to face our fears head-on. In the book and movie trilogy Divergent, a story about a dystopian society where people are categorized based on personal qualities, the characters identified as "brave" are given challenges where they are forced to face their biggest fears to demonstrate courage. They are placed in simulations where they lose the ability to distinguish fantasy from reality and must conquer their fear by realizing that what they perceive to be a threat is only an illusion. The key to their freedom is to move toward their nightmare rather than to retreat. They are required to look their own devil in the eye to be free.

Facing what scares us is like exposing the wizard in *The Wizard of Oz*. Fear itself is often exponentially worse than the reality of our demon. We have all experienced this. Perhaps you can recall a time when you were scared to ask your boss for a raise and felt a rush of adrenaline afterward. Maybe you were terrified of going on a roller coaster with your child but ended up loving it so much, you immediately got back in line. Asking someone on a date, giving a speech, or starting to exercise after years of stagnation are other examples of facing our fears. The courage it takes to do what feels like swimming upstream is precisely what positions us to swim downstream. Said another way, the only way out is in. Brené Brown says,

"Only when we are brave enough to explore the darkness will we discover the infinite power of our light." Facing our fears does not guarantee the outcome we hope for, but it does guarantee serious badassery.

During my recovery I had plenty of practice dealing with unwanted experiences. This included health issues, relationship challenges, perceived failures of many kinds, and parenting dilemmas. At some point I realized that difficulties were not simply evidence my life was hard, but instead were opportunities to practice transcending my limitations and develop resiliency. This realization marked a shift from victimhood to empowerment. I will not say I am excited when life tests me, but I'm now pretty good at navigating undesirable experiences. When I'm challenged, I now realize that the difficulty at hand is the gateway to more emotional freedom once I heal the original wound that is being revealed by the challenge.

Two of my noteworthy experiences in resiliency building were associated with car predicaments. My oldest daughter and I had a tradition of going shopping on Labor Day weekend in the Kansas City area, about seventy-five minutes from where we live. The years I did not feel well enough to do this on my own, my husband chauffeured us. One year, I felt I had the stamina to take her by myself but was uncertain, so we decided to make it a short day to ensure our success. When we were done with our shopping, my daughter elected to drive us home. As we headed back, a tire on our car blew. Fortunately, my daughter was able to pull over safely. I initially felt some panic, as it was clear a quick fix was unlikely and I wasn't sure I had the physical stamina to handle this unexpected event.

I had been studying the law of attraction and strengthening my mindset, so I knew that how I handled this adversity was important. I quickly focused on ease. I called AAA, an emergency roadside assistance company. Then a helpful stranger who worked at a tire shop pulled over to help, and the AAA professional arrived a short time later. I was pleased and felt confident my optimism was paying off—until I was told we would not be able to drive home on the emergency tire. We were directed to a tire repair shop, but it was late in the day, and I worried the shop would soon close. I took a breath and worked to shift my fear to optimism. It was forced, but I got some momentum going.

The shop we were initially steered toward did not have the tire we needed. We moved on. The next shop did not have time to fit us in. We tried again. After traveling very slowly because of our emergency tire, we found a repair shop on our fifth try. It had the tire we needed and the time to replace our temporary tire with a very solid new tire. The elation we felt when we finally got our new tire and headed home was unforgettable. I told my husband the high cost of the tire was worth every penny because it was an important and memorable resiliency-building experience for both my daughter and me.

Another example of growth through adversity occurred as the result of a car accident I had when I was in St. Louis for a professional training. I was still dealing with a lot of health symptoms, and it was a stretch for me to make this trip on my own. I arrived in St. Louis after a long drive, feeling very tired. It was late, dark, and rainy, and I was in an unfamiliar area. The accident was fairly minor, but I was terribly sore. I had to deal with a series of challenges in the aftermath of the accident, including talking with police and EMTs, getting to my hotel, having my car towed, finding transportation to and from my training each day, and recovering physically from the crash.

I had previously read Peter Levine's book *In an Unspoken Voice*, where he describes how he responded after he was hit in a crosswalk. He describes precisely what he did to prevent himself from developing PTSD, and I mimicked what he did as much as I could. Since social support is a major factor in ameliorating trauma reactions, I let a supportive, kind bystander who happened to be a nurse stay with me at the scene. I also allowed my body to discharge the survival energy from the accident, which I had learned in my training in Somatic Experiencing. I asked the police officers to wait to interview me until I was ready. I called my friend Jennifer from St. Louis, who helped me get to my hotel and lovingly provided the support I needed. My husband handled as many details as he could from home. I also attended the four-day Somatic Experiencing training I was there for and received an unbelievable amount of support.

Getting through this trial allowed me to exercise the muscles of acceptance, surrender, and appreciation. I was given the opportunity to see how strong and resilient I was becoming. I was also very well supported during this stressful time, which enabled me to see that the world was a friendly and helpful place. I know not everyone may have this kind of ideal scenario after a car accident, but as I reflected on why things went so smoothly for me, I recognized I was given such vast support because I allowed myself to receive it.

Even if I had been unsuccessful at handling these challenges, I would have grown. If we are not winning, we are learning. When we feel disappointed in an outcome or in how we navigated difficulty, we gain information that impacts how we navigate future challenges. We will always have plenty of practice to improve our ability to deal with obstacles. If we don't feel we dealt with something ideally, we are guaranteed more opportunities to try again. We are here to grow and evolve. Difficulties provide the catalysts we need. Surrendering to this fact of life can allow us to embrace difficulty, further shoring up our capacity to be empowered.

Pillar 3

Vision

M any adults who grew up without enough love, connection, and affection have come to expect very little from life. The imprint of powerlessness and helplessness from childhood makes it difficult for many of us to truly believe we can experience a fulfilling life. Because of this, many wounded people settle for far less than they desire.

When I begin my work with people recovering from childhood trauma, I often ask them what they really want out of life. I ask how they would like to feel and what they long for in relationships with others. I challenge them to consider where they want to live, how they want to live, and what kinds of life experiences they want to enjoy. Often people cannot immediately answer these questions. At some point, many traumatized people stop dreaming and yearning for a fulfilling life because it was too painful to want something they believed was out of reach. They learned to limit the possibility of feeling disappointed and deprived.

Please know that even if they are hidden, you do have hopes and dreams. When you have experiences that you do not want, a desire is sparked, revealing what you do want. Abraham, affectionately known as Abe Hicks, is the nonphysical consciousness channeled by Esther Hicks; they teach this principle in the book *Ask and It Is Given*. Together they explain that the benefit of "contrast," or undesirable experiences, causes us to shoot rockets of desire toward a more optimal alternative. For example, the lack of love felt growing up initiates a deep hunger to be loved, cherished, and adored. Living in poverty creates a wish for financial security. A childhood without friendships sparks a longing for meaningful relationships. Living in a dirty home can ignite a desire for a beautiful, warm home. Hopelessness may have suppressed our desires, but awakening our dreams can motivate us to achieve the peace and abundance for which we truly long.

I wrote the acknowledgment section of my doctoral dissertation before I even began my research, thanking all who helped me. When we begin with the end in mind, it can help us progress in life with more determination and confidence.

Early in the therapy process I invite my clients to make a list of desires. Some people create a vision board with a collage of pictures representing their wants. A visual representation of goals and dreams, viewed regularly, can spark hope as it chips away at the expectation of lack and bad luck.

I once heard Bessel van der Kolk, MD, say that we must have a capacity to visualize something to bring it into existence. When we identify the ideals for our life, the contemplation and focus required to construct our vision can produce the eagerness and motivation necessary to move forward. Establishing a vision helps propel our fantasies into a potential reality. Simply considering the possibility of fulfilling our desires gets the ball rolling. Momentum is good.

It can take an incredible amount of tenacity to stick to a healing plan. Healing involves agreeing to a lifestyle that limits various forms of negativity, including what we eat, drink, read, and watch, and with whom we spend time. Healing requires a commitment to daily practices, which may include meditation, gentle exercise, rest, self-love practices, and journaling. It may also mean we attend weekly therapy sessions and meet regularly with bodyworkers or energy healers. The key is to commit to doing whatever it takes to be free of past trauma. It is a process of saying yes to what leads to expansion and no to what causes constriction. It is not always easy to have the discipline it takes to heal. Developing a vision for our life can aid us in aligning our daily decisions with success.

Before I was committed to healing, I was addicted to watching shows depicting dark and troubled characters, including *Dexter*, *Breaking Bad*, and *Dateline*. Early in my healing journey I knew these shows only enhanced the bleakness I felt because they promoted a relationship with darkness and confirmed my bias that the world was not a safe place. Despite my initial longing to continue watching them, I knew I had to remove all negativity from my life if I wanted to heal. This required sacrifice, but my commitment to well-being was more important than my dark TV drama addiction. Creating the vision I wanted for my life helped me stick to the limits I needed to place on myself to recover.

I included the following desires in the vision I have held for many years:

- Being in a loving, mutually respectful partner relationship
- Being a loving, present, and nurturing parent
- Enjoying friendships with like-minded people
- Having a healthy and fit body
- Having fulfilling work and making a positive contribution to others
- Being emotionally, physically, mentally, and spiritually healthy
- Enjoying travels to unique locations with loved ones

- Being free from my past
- Financial abundance
- Capacity to easily surrender

Reverend Amy Roden, teacher for the Berkeley Psychic Institute, taught me about *havingness*, a word and concept I love. Receiving is difficult for people with a trauma background. When we grow up in deficient circumstances, our template for receiving is limited and prevents us from allowing ourselves to "have" what we would really like.

My acupuncturist taught me about yin deficiency, which is essentially the Chinese medicine version of havingness. How much can we allow ourselves to receive? If we can receive, can we also keep what we have received? You've probably heard stories of people who have won the lottery only to lose all their winnings in short order.

It is necessary to know what we want in life, but that alone won't bring our desires to us and allow us to keep them once we have them. We must be a vibrational match to our desires, which we accomplish by addressing our beliefs. If you want a healthy and fit body but hate the way you look, you may sabotage any efforts to achieve the physical wellness you crave. If you do not have satisfying work, it may be because you hold beliefs that oppose your ability to be fulfilled professionally. If you are fearful, it is because you fundamentally believe you are not safe in the world. To have what we want, we must change our paradigm of lack and limitation, by clearing out shame, blame, and unworthiness. When we are in alignment with our Essence, receiving and keeping is easy.

Once in the middle of the night I slipped on the stairs as I was going to get some water. It wasn't pretty. I instantly knew I was going to be hurting for a while. My husband came to check on me. I told him to put his hands on my shoulders where I detected the injury. Within moments, the pain was completely gone. I intuitively knew what I needed for an instant recovery, and I could let myself have and keep the healing.

Healing our trauma enables our belief system to change, allowing us to come into alignment with our greatest desires. This puts us in contact with Essence, the part of us that knows our mission in life and gives the final stamp of approval on what we bring into our lives and what we do not. Holding the vision for what we want can motivate us to do the hard work it takes to heal trauma and shift our beliefs. I encourage you to consider what you would want for your life if there were no limitations. Aim high. You deserve a vibrant and happy life.

Pillar 4

Know Your Story

Developing a coherent narrative is a major milestone in healing trauma. This means that we have gained awareness of our life story and are able to process, understand, and accept the entirety of what has transpired. Knowing our story enables us to develop what is known as an *earned secure* attachment in which we transform from a wounded person into someone who ultimately feels capable and safe. With a coherent narrative and a secure attachment we are connected to our Essence and can navigate the ups and downs in life with confidence. A major task necessary in the development of internal coherence, and in thus restoring wholeness, is the willingness to know the truth about what we have experienced in life, even if it is painful.

When we move toward reconnection with our true self, our life story unfolds one layer at a time. It is important to allow the past to surface naturally rather than seek recovery of repressed memories. Working only with memories as they arise allows trauma work to be titrated, that is, to come in doses we can handle without becoming terribly overwhelmed.

There may not be explicit memories for every part of childhood, particularly for people whose trauma is more extreme. This was certainly the case for me. As a graduate student, training as a therapist, I learned that lack of access to childhood memories was a likely indicator of trauma. This felt eerie to me, as I had very few childhood memories. As I learned more about trauma and recovery, I began to feel like there was a storm brewing that I could not see but knew was on the way, which ended up being the case. This was my intuition at work, beginning to prepare me for the path ahead, where memories of abuse would one day surface.

Many of us recall facts about childhood as we become more capable of digesting what happened. This doesn't mean we don't feel scared and overwhelmed when trauma memories surface. Flashbacks, whether visual or emotional, make us feel like the trauma is happening right now. We may initially want to bury our head in the sand or take another dose of emotional anesthesia.

Just like becoming a parent or losing a loved one, there is no way to be fully prepared for the emergence of a challenging reality. The truth about our past may arise spontaneously after conversations with others who have a similar history or during a therapy or Reiki or other energy healing session. Memories of childhood trauma can surface while meditating, or when an occurrence in life mirrors our original traumas to us, such as watching a movie with an abuse scene. One person I knew had no memories of childhood trauma until they surfaced during the aftermath of a traumatic car accident. In whatever form the veil lifts and the truth about our past returns to us, we can be sure that it happens when our higher self decides it is time.

I have worked with many clients who experienced sexual dissatisfaction with their partners. They found sex to be frustrating, confusing, unpleasant, painful, and unwanted. Although there can be many reasons for a person to be sexually challenged, one cause is a history of sexual abuse. In some cases, a person has no conscious memory of sexual trauma because the memories have been repressed. When we have repressed sexual trauma, we can be confused about our lack of ability to experience sexual pleasure and often think there is something fundamentally wrong with us and our body.

Sexual trauma produces a long-term response in the human body, which has many avenues for preventing further sexual victimization. We can feel repulsed by closeness with our partners, as the body may not be able to differentiate a safe partner from our abuser. Our body can turn off sexual responsiveness and can also use pain as a deterrent. We may unconsciously sabotage a budding relationship for fear of the expectation of sex.

It's challenging enough to deal with the aftermath of a sexual trauma when we recall what happened, but when it is hidden from our conscious view, we can feel even more confused and sexually inadequate. Recovering awareness of sexual abuse can be particularly complicated. Even after many years of healing myself, new details regarding my own sexual trauma surfaced from time to time. Even though it was not easy to recall the trauma, there was relief in knowing what I had been through, because it helped me make sense of the struggles I had faced in my adult life. For people with a history of sexual trauma, uncovering our story takes a good deal of patience and kindness toward ourselves and from our partners.

When repressed trauma memories surface, we may feel a combination of relief and shock. We can experience relief as the memories, like puzzle pieces, fall into place, finally allowing us to make more sense of a complicated life. Shock can reflect disbelief about the reality of our history of abuse. Once our denial lifts, it can feel obvious that the criticism, judgment, hostility, neglect, and other forms of mistreatment from parents hurt us.

Why don't some of us remember our trauma? Aside from the coping skill of denial and the self-doubt that comes from gaslighting, we are disconnected from our story because we cannot be fully embodied when we are under high levels of stress. Our subconscious mind kindly blocks access to highly traumatic information, and our spirit leaves the body when pain is too great. When we are not present in our body, we are not capable of completely remembering overwhelming experiences, though they are never truly forgotten.

It is empowering to know our story. Knowledge gives us understanding and choice. Until we are in touch with what we experienced in childhood, life can be complicated and confusing. It is an unsolved mystery.

For example, Natalie always felt unsettled in late October. She had no idea why, but we intended to figure it out. We worked with her implicit memory by connecting with the body sensations associated with her anxiety. This enabled her to access a repressed memory of her father holding her family at gunpoint one Halloween when she was young. Using Somatic Experiencing, we assisted her in bringing this trauma to completion. She felt a tremendous relief of symptoms and finally understood why she had always hated Halloween.

In another example, Caroline was fearful of saying the wrong thing to women in our developmental trauma recovery group. As we worked to understand the origin of this fear, she recalled an experience as a young adult when she innocently asked a panicked relative whose son was injured if she was okay. Caroline's father overheard this exchange and berated her for asking "such a stupid question." By uncovering a core memory associated with Caroline's fear of saying the wrong thing, she was able to begin freeing herself from it. She went on to more confidently express herself in the group and support other women in a meaningful way.

Knowing our story can make us less judgmental of ourselves.

I heard a quote at a play therapy training many years ago and it stayed with me: "If we knew all, all could be forgiven." I have consistently found this to hold true; if I felt judgmental toward someone but learned about their story, my criticism disappeared. Everyone's behavior makes more sense when we understand what they have been through. The same was true of my own self-criticism. It became much easier to forgive myself for perceived mistakes and regrets as I came to understand my own story. I let go of the need to beat myself up and instead started to see myself as strong and courageous.

Although knowing our story is empowering, it is important to resist the temptation to over-identify with our story. Over-identifying means we excessively, and without objectivity, identify ourselves as being traumatized and disregard other aspects of who we are. We are not what happened to us. We are not our illness, our emotions, or our trauma. Using language such as "my abuse" and "my trauma" allows the consequences of our past to dominate our life. When we over-identify with our abuse history, we spend our time thinking about what happened to us and stay hyper-focused on trauma symptoms.

Recognizing my own tendency to over-identify with my experiences, I had to address the question "Who will I be if I am not consumed by pain?" Physical pain had been present in my life, defining what I could and could not do for thirty years. I had lived with it longer that I had lived without it, and it had become a defining feature of my life. It was such a consuming part of my identity that I didn't even realize the degree to which I had over-identified with it. Trauma recovery requires us to have both understanding and respect for what we have been through while not allowing it to define us.

Another advantage of knowing our story and working toward internal coherence is that we can begin to recall good parts of our childhood. In some cases, there can be very little reprieve during a tough childhood, but most people have some bright spots. I now have memories of my mom throwing birthday parties for us. She planned games and made decorative cakes. I have memories of my dad helping me study for tests in elementary school and running with me to help me train when I was a track athlete. Until I had some level of healing from the extensive abuse at the hands of my parents, I could not appreciate the times they did not fail me.

I have known many people who did not want to know their story. They did not want to open what they believed was Pandora's box. However, our story is playing out in our everyday life, reflected in difficult relationships, anxiety, lack of direction, and pretty much any other discordant area of our life. Our choice is whether we want to bring consciousness to our story or would rather unconsciously engage in trauma reenactments, ignoring our suppressed pain.

Our Essence will continue to bring opportunities for us to know our story. This is a necessary part of our healing and is required for returning us to wholeness. I invite you to surrender your fears of the unknowns of your past and see that there is tremendous freedom in knowing your story and therefore in developing your coherent narrative. It is true: The truth does set you free when you are ready.

Pillar 5

Embrace Your Spiritual Self

I use a variety of terms to refer to the Divine, including Supreme Being, Creator, Universe, Universal Intelligence, and God. I do not believe the name matters, though others may feel differently. That's okay. Whatever we call the Divine, we likely agree that this holy presence is the creative life force that connects everything. As we open ourselves to spirituality, we see the Divine within ourselves, which ultimately can allow us to see our own perfection and the perfection of life.

Spirituality is a practice, or way of being, whereby we acknowledge that everyone and everything is connected. When we are aligned with our Essence, we know we are more than our bodies and personalities. We know there is a plan, and that we are never alone. We believe there is no real death, because we are infinite beings. Through spirituality we can trust we are supported and guided, and that "all is well," even if it doesn't seem to be.

Spirituality can offer relief when we feel emotionally and physically burdened, although many traumatized adults who were hurt by their parents resist it. Parents are God-like to children, and when they hurt them, children distrust not only their parents, but God as well. Trauma shatters a person's belief that there is an order to life and that someone or something is in charge.

I was angry with God for a long time. My expectations of God reflected the relationship with my dad. He was judgmental, absent, controlling, and undependable. I believed God was the same. It was tormenting to have both a longing for and anger toward God. This went on for years until one day, near the height of my health crisis, my gentle and compassionate massage therapist Susan said, "Mindi, God loves you." Her sincere desire to help me combined with my desperateness was enough to finally soften my resistance to reconnecting with the Divine.

Shortly after this encounter, I was led to Gary Zukav's book *The Seat of the Soul.* I learned about karma, intuition, and personal power. I began to understand more about my human experience as a journey in which I was meant to align with my soul in the quest to transform my life. Inspired, I realized for the first time that I could change my own life. Zukav's book offered me a profound awakening, and it was a relief to have a helpful framework to understand human suffering.

A spiritual awakening can be very uncomfortable. We can feel a heightened sense of suffering related to being lost, alone, confused, depressed, and overwhelmed as the insulation, or denial, about our pain is removed. We can feel very alone and disconnected from God, lost, and unable to make sense of difficult life experiences. This leads to what is known as the *dark night of the soul.* Eckhart Tolle, who is known for his spontaneous spiritual awakening, describes the dark night of the soul on his website:

> It is a term used to describe what one could call a collapse of a perceived meaning in life . . . an eruption into your life of a deep sense of meaninglessness. The inner state in some cases is very close to what is conventionally called depression. Nothing makes sense anymore, there's no purpose to anything. Sometimes it's triggered by some external event, some disaster perhaps. . . The meaning that you had given

your life, your activities, your achievements, where you are going, what is considered important . . . for some reason collapses. . .Often it is part of the awakening process, the death of the old self and the birth of the true self.

What causes a dark night of the soul? For many people, including me, this happens when the culmination of pain related to childhood trauma reaches a critical mass and suppression is no longer a viable option. Trying to pass as "normal" becomes impossible. A dark night of the soul is synonymous with the transformational journey. This peak of misery provides a fork in the road: Stay unhappy or heal. Dark nights reflect a person's disconnection from Essence and provide the impetus toward reconnection.

Spiritual awakening is essentially the process of learning to live an intentional and aware life instead of being driven by childhood and societal programming. Many spiritual teachers explain that trauma is a pathway to personal evolution. For most people there is little motivation to grow when we feel too comfortable, which is why most deep personal growth follows tragedy. Painful experiences often make us more receptive to growth. Hardship guarantees that our connection to higher power is tested, which can open a door we had previously closed.

Waking up can be uncomfortable. We become more aware of suffering in the world, and are asked to end unproductive relationships, make a variety of life changes, and face a painful past. Though it can be a grueling process, it is the path to freedom, the means by which to reconnect with our Essence. Here are some signs that you are awakening:

- **Feeling a greater connection to all things.** When we begin to feel more unity, we embrace the concept of oneness, the idea we are all connected. This makes way for less judgment and more compassion.

- **Becoming more intuitive.** People often experience heightened intuition. For example, you may be thinking about someone just before they call or understand what someone else is feeling or thinking. For some this can feel overwhelming, so learning to use your specific intuitive skills will help normalize them, making them as ordinary as your physical senses.
- **Being drawn to nature.** An awakened person begins to appreciate the beauty and power of nature.
- **Achieving a more expanded perspective.** You will become less self-absorbed and more concerned with topics that affect the greater good. You become more interested in living responsibly, being a good steward of the Earth, and helping those who are exploited and oppressed. Until you learn to come from your heart, you may feel more angered and outraged about injustice.
- **Becoming more interested in "being" instead of "doing."** Awakening helps you be less driven by accomplishment and more by quality of life.
- **Developing self-acceptance.** You learn to stop criticizing yourself and love yourself more. You engage less in people-pleasing behavior and more in living authentically.
- **Having increased feelings of inner peace.** Releasing the pain of the past allows you to feel freer. You live for yourself instead of others.
- **Being more present.** Instead of being depressed about the past and worried about the future, you learn to live in the now.
- **Seeking more meaning in life.** You are no longer satisfied with a mundane life. Instead, you seek richness and expansion and you want to contribute to others.

- **Feeling like you do not fit in.** You can no longer tolerate superficial conversations and relationships and instead seek out people who can engage in deep, meaningful conversations. You disconnect from people who do not understand you.

- **Taking more responsibility for your life.** You realize that you are the creator of your life experiences and accept the task of being more intentional in your focus.

- **Noticing signs and synchronicities.** You notice recurring numbers such as 111, 222, and my personal favorite, 333. You receive similar messages from multiple sources that seem like coincidences, except there are no coincidences.

- **Desiring to take better care of yourself.** You pay more attention to what you eat, what media you use, and how you spend your time.

- **Being judgmental toward others who are not awakening.** As you begin to look at life with a more open perspective, you may initially be more critical of those who do not.

- **Working through past traumas.** You now face unresolved traumatic experiences instead of avoiding them. It can be difficult to have your numbing agents removed, but you courageously address your wounds.

Seeking answers to the mysteries of life will help us resolve our suffering. In the quest to know why they have been harmed, some of my clients find satisfaction in concluding that although God does not cause bad things to happen, all experiences can be used for good. For others, coming to terms with complex victimization requires a deeper dive into spirituality. Learning about advanced spiritual concepts such as karma, past lives, pre-birth planning, soul retrieval, and soul contracts can help us make sense of why we have experienced what we have. This was the case for me.

I immersed myself in many complex aspects of spirituality. Desperate for answers my whole life, I felt as if I'd been resurrected, or brought back to life, as I uncovered the truth about why we experience hardship. Learning how my own karma influenced my life experiences made me feel less of a victim. I also felt more empowered when I realized that I set up many conditions of my life before I was born. For example, it has been profoundly difficult for me to deal with intense and long-standing body pain. It felt less punishing when I learned that I chose this pain because it assured that I would achieve the level of personal growth I intended for this life. I came to see that my pain had a noble purpose, which allowed for more acceptance.

I am certain that when we seek answers with sincerity and persistence, we find the information we need. Sometimes this takes a while, but at other times answers come immediately. Many years ago, I watched an upsetting episode of *a* popular news program that profiled triplet infants who had been seriously abused and neglected by their troubled parents. I repeatedly asked God in the following days, "Why would you give these babies to people who had no business being parents?"

This unconsciously mirrored my question about why I was given to my impaired parents. I vividly recall one day hearing God respond, "That's why I sent you." At the time I did not fully understand what this meant, but I felt an unmistakable calm.

It made more sense to me in the following months as I sought an internship to finish up my degree. Though I was not initially interested in being a child therapist, the only position I could find was at a mental health center working with kids.

I found I loved working with traumatized children and over the years pursued extensive training with Dr. Dan Hughes, a world-renowned attachment and trauma expert, who was an invaluable mentor to me. As I worked with traumatized children, the message from God that day made more sense. The trauma I experienced uniquely prepared me to be a dedicated and compassionate therapist for traumatized children and their families. This work has been an integral part of my life mission.

Reconnecting with our spirit is how we improve every aspect of our lives. Our Essence is always guiding us toward integration, making way for us to align with our life mission. When we are united with our Essence, we approach life with a sense of ease and surrender. Our ego becomes quieter, and resistance retreats. Alignment with our inner being relies on our dedication to return to wholeness, where we ultimately discard the illusion of ourselves as broken and separate from all that is. The dark night of the soul is replaced with a beautiful life.

Pillar 6

Acceptance

Michael Singer, author of the book *The Surrender Experiment*, said, "No wonder there is so much tension, anxiety, and fear. Each of us actually believes that things should be the way we want them, instead of being the natural result of all the forces of creation" (p. 4).

Acceptance is the place we arrive at when we have released the yearning for life to be what it is not. It means we have let go of the ache for a future that hasn't happened yet, and we no longer blindly believe in truths that do not exist. Additionally, we trust that emotional and physical pain are avenues for healing our original wounds, our tickets to freedom. And those of us who are willing to take complete responsibility for our lives trust that our past and current struggles are perfect for our soul growth.

Acceptance is the process where, bit by bit, we come to terms with what has happened to us and the state of our current lives. In the here and now, we are present with what we are experiencing, without resistance. This can be a challenge for those recovering from developmental trauma, because when we have been wounded, we naturally want things to be different from how they were and are. There was a lot of pain when we were being hurt, and there's a lot of pain in the aftermath as we live with the consequences stemming from abuse and neglect. The memories, thoughts, and sensations that arise are uncomfortable, and we understandably don't like them.

Our attachment to our position prevents acceptance. We may have strong feelings that what someone did to us was wrong and that they should take responsibility. We may want to see them punished and to suffer as we have. We may long to be free of pain, illness, and financial limitations. We may wish for healthy relationships, a successful job, a fit body, and we can feel angry when these wishes feel out of reach. However, we cannot change what happened. If we continue to invest our energy in unchangeable facts, we will suffer. The inability to let go of the past and to accept our current life circumstances fuels resentment, which leads to bitterness. It is impossible to be both bitter and happy.

Acceptance does not mean we were not hurt. Or that we are glad we experienced what we did. It means we are no longer overly focused on the pain of our past. It means we have come to a satisfactory understanding about why we experienced trauma, and we are no longer stuck feeling resentful and disappointed, and blaming those who hurt us.

A scene in the series finale of the show *Transparent* poignantly illustrates acceptance. This show is about three adult children and the difficulties they experience after being raised by parents with complex personality challenges. In the scene there's a reception in the family home after the funeral service for one parent. An elderly woman asks one of the daughters, "Did you have a good childhood in this home?" The siblings share knowing glances with each other before the character Alexandra Pfefferman pauses and says confidently, "It made me who I am." This is a hallmark of healing: making peace with the challenges and adversity we faced growing up.

My husband is very good at this. He is a preacher's kid. His family moved several times, which meant he faced challenges being the new kid in town. Now he sees the value of these difficult childhood experiences. He has a unique gift of being able to get along with everyone, and he thanks his nomadic upbringing for this ability.

Achieving a state of acceptance is multifaceted. We must move from resistance, denial, and anger, where we are filled with tension and rigidity, to acknowledgment, surrender, and, ultimately, letting go, which relies on us to relax. This takes commitment, persistence, and know-how.

One of the first steps toward acceptance is acknowledging what we have been through. This involves conceding that we *were* hurt by our parents or others. We let go of the denial that protected us from the pain, release the false narrative of a happy family, and acknowledge the reality of our difficult childhood and our suffering. When we do this, we begin the process of acceptance.

Once we can acknowledge what we have experienced, we can allow ourselves to get in touch with all the feelings associated with being hurt. No matter how spiritual we are, we cannot bypass the anger that results from being betrayed by our parents and others. When resentment, anger, disappointment, grief, and hatred surface, it is an acknowledgment that we have been wronged. I personally felt I had a bottomless pit of anger that took a considerable amount of time to work through, even though I did not want to be angry and resentful toward my parents. There was simply no way around it. But even though outrage is a necessary precursor to acceptance, it cannot be permanent for cycle breakers. We get stuck when we are unable to release blame toward those who hurt us. Healing requires acknowledgment of pain and trauma while also working to let it go.

I once had a Reiki session in which I was told by the practitioner, "Spirit is telling me you need to let go." I did not know what this meant. Throughout the treatment, I kept asking, "Am I letting go?" Sometime later, another intuitive healer told me the same thing. I still did not understand. I felt I could not be more committed to my recovery, and it didn't make sense to me that I was not "letting go."

I turned to Google for answers: "How do you let go?" I learned in my search that *acceptance* is a requirement for letting go. I suddenly realized that although I felt I had come to terms with how I had been raised, I had not accepted the aftermath: the pain, limitations, illness, isolation, and being chronically misunderstood. I desperately wanted to feel good and have the freedoms that seemed so natural for others. The truth was, I was traumatized and physically limited, and no amount of anger and frustration could change that.

With this new understanding I committed to letting go of the desire for my life to be any different. I finally understood that acceptance was a requirement for feeling good. I began regularly citing the Serenity Prayer, listening to meditations about letting go, feeling gratitude for the beauty and ease I did have, and focusing on all I had learned through the challenges I had faced instead of the limitations they brought. I engaged in a daily acceptance practice where I expressed love for myself, my body, my pain, and my inner child, and showered myself with compassion. I discovered that intense chronic pain resulted from my body holding the emotions and tension from childhood so I could function. I finally realized my body was not against me and that instead it had been my faithful companion. The insights and relief I felt were helpful in my journey toward acceptance, but they alone were not enough. The deeper work required for acceptance was learning to identify when I was in a state of resistance and then healing the original wounds that were responsible for my struggle.

When we can accept how we feel and also move toward the root of why we are suffering, we create opportunities for healing. The key is knowing how to use distress as the gateway to a better life. When we are distressed, there is always a part of us we are rejecting, the part that is lacking love and integration. Our task is to access this part, bring completion to the unhealed trauma, transform the limiting beliefs associated with it, and integrate our fragmented parts. Our wounded inner child leaves bread crumbs for us (although it sometimes feels like a whole loaf) through emotional and physical discomfort. When we follow the clues, we can use this information to heal our original wounds.

A client once asked me, "Is it wrong to wish for things?" I explained that wishing can cause suffering by limiting our acceptance of what is. Although it's not wrong to wish for things, we feel better when we can release our attachment and longing for what is currently out of reach. A wish that a relationship had not ended, that we had taken a job we passed up, or that we had been treated differently by our parents takes us out of the present moment and makes it difficult to enjoy our life. If we want to feel good, it is important to surrender the longing for our wishes.

This is different from confidently setting goals for ourselves. In goal setting, we can accept what is while also working toward what we want. This is not striving, longing, or wishing; it is the process of implementation.

Take an inventory of how you feel about your life. When you think about your past, health, relationships, financial state, and how you feel when you look in the mirror, where do you feel resistance? What do you reject? Be honest, but also be gentle. This exercise can show you areas of your life that need acceptance. What is blocking you from being okay with your life? What would it be like to embrace how you feel and look, and what you have experienced? This exploration can uncover what is preventing you from experiencing the peace you desire. When you identify barriers such as "I just can't let go of the anger toward my father for what he did to me," or "My mom loved my brother more," you have helpful targets for therapeutic intervention.

Eckhart Tolle teaches us to accept what is, in the present moment. Maybe we cannot accept the entire painful situation, but perhaps we can find acceptance for right now. Acceptance in the here and now moves us out of the past and pulls us back from the future. Like all elements of trauma recovery, acceptance is a process. Be kind with yourself. When you are in pain, acknowledge and validate yourself, feel your feels, and when you are ready, give yourself permission to let go.

Though acceptance takes time, it is achievable for anyone who remains committed to transcending suffering and breaking the cycle.

Trust

Do you have a difficult time accepting compliments? Do people tell you that you are wonderful, but you don't believe them? Do you long for more in your life but believe that you are destined for smallness? Do you feel scared . . . a lot?

Lack of trust in ourselves, in others, and in life itself is often at the heart of living an unfulfilled life. We limit ourselves because the fear involved in being seen, depending on others, and taking chances sometimes feels insurmountable and not worth the risk. This template of distrust was created when we did not feel safe as kids.

Children are at the mercy of the adults in charge. When parents mistreat them, children feel a total loss of power over their lives and can develop learned helplessness as a result. This means they are so convinced they cannot get their needs met that they stop trying. When children experience betrayal from parents, they develop beliefs such as "I don't trust myself," "No one can help me," "I can't count on anyone," and "Something bad is going to happen." They feel ineffective at life. Betrayal by parents often removes the possibility that children can trust anyone, including themselves. This forms the basis for our global lack of trust and the subsequent need to control.

Distrust can create a desire for dominance over others. Living with a dictator or being neglected by an absent parent prompts some children to want to be the powerful one in a relationship.

They may conclude there are only two roles in life: being dominant or being dominated. This is one origin of bullying.

People try to control life to satisfy their desperation to avoid more pain and loss. Control only gives a false sense of safety, though, because people with unhealed trauma never can feel completely safe. Nor is it possible for them to have complete certainty about safety. In my own recovery I struggled with how to feel safe, given the lingering possibility something else traumatic could occur. Life is full of uncertainty.

Relative safety is the phrase Peter Levine uses to define the possibility of safety for any human. There is no guarantee we will never be hurt again. We must acknowledge but not dwell on the fact that bad things may still happen. As we heal ourselves, we limit our potential for abuse from others. As we develop confidence, uncertainty feels less threatening.

We feel more trust in life as we connect to our Essence. This connection enables us to know we are *eternally* safe, regardless of what happens here on Earth. Even if we have experienced nearly unbearable trauma, we do not suffer without purpose. Our true safety lies in the fact that everything, no matter how difficult, is Divinely allowed; therefore, even tragic circumstances benefit our highest good. An unwanted injury can slow down the workaholic, and the death of an inspirational person can inspire others to pick up the torch. The ending of a difficult relationship can make room for the love of your life. There are countless examples of how a hardship can lead us to a much better life.

Strengthening trust requires mindfulness. That means being aware of our thoughts, emotions, and behavior, which helps us notice when we are attempting to control life. At times I still find myself being a bit bossy or controlling with my husband, but we typically have a playful attitude about it, because I often catch myself in the act and he is not shy about kindly pointing it out. Mindfulness also allows us to spot the evidence that life is supporting us.

Mindfulness helps us notice instead of discount the help we receive. One night I was having a difficult time sleeping because of physical pain. After unsuccessfully trying to help myself feel better, I reached for my husband. He held me and said the Serenity Prayer, and I was instantly soothed. The physical pain did not change, but my distress about it did, which helped me. This was concrete evidence that my needs were met. How often do we miss the signs that life provides the support we need? We can see only what we are willing to see. We can receive only what we allow ourselves to receive.

We can cultivate trust in life as we lessen our tendency to judge an experience as bad or good. Judgment is a survival skill originating from the need to routinely assess threats in childhood. Our brain becomes a survival overachiever, so we need to retrain it. Practicing nonjudgment is one way to do this. The Taoist Parable of the Chinese Farmer, made popular by writer Alan Watts, illustrates the value of nonjudgment.

> Once upon a time there was a Chinese farmer whose horse ran away. That evening, all of his neighbors came around to commiserate. They said, "We are sorry to see your horse has run away. This is most unfortunate." The farmer replied, "Maybe."
>
> The next day, the horse came back bringing seven wild horses with it, and in the evening everybody came back and said, "Oh, isn't that lucky, what a great turn of events. You now have eight horses." The farmer again said, "Maybe."
>
> The following day, his son tried to break one of the horses, and while riding it, was thrown and broke his leg. The neighbors then said, "Oh dear, that's too bad," and the farmer replied, "Maybe."

The next day, the conscription officers came around to conscript people into the army and rejected his son because he had a broken leg. Again, all of the neighbors came around and said, "Isn't that great." Again, he said, "Maybe."

After trauma, cynicism can be our default response to hardship. We simply do not trust that things will easily work out or that we will have the help we need. At the first sign of difficulty we can feel discouraged because we believe, based on our history of trauma, that more pain is on the way. This parable teaches us to suspend judgment about the meaning of an event, trusting that whatever is happening in the moment is not the whole story.

Developing a sense of safety in life happens naturally as we heal from trauma, but we can also intentionally work to cultivate the capacity for trust. We can learn to avoid untrustworthy people and circumstances and to trust people and situations that are trustworthy.

For example, Jana felt betrayed by life. She had grown up with extreme trauma and was angry and never fully felt safe. One day I encouraged her to list all the ways her needs were currently met despite all she had been through. She had not recognized that the social support, mentoring, and financial help she was freely provided by her community was evidence that she was being given what she needed. Her tunnel vision had been disabling because it allowed her to focus only on what had not been provided in the past. This change in awareness helped her become more observant of the fact that she now had many trustworthy people in her life.

Perhaps you could try this. List how you are being supported in your life. Who or what have you overlooked as a resource or an ally?

Another trust-building practice is to talk to, write letters to, or journal to the Divine. We can express our anger and confusion as well as desires and hopes. We can ask questions and make requests. The book *Conversations with God* began as Neale Donald Walsch wrote a letter to God in which he angrily expressed his frustrations about life. In the dialogue with God that followed he suddenly and unexpectedly began to receive detailed answers to his questions. These lengthy conversations spanned many years and led to a masterpiece series of books that hold profound wisdom.

We can intentionally work to develop more trust by making it a practice to set good boundaries, get in touch with our wants and needs, be kind and gentle with ourselves, and allow only others who do the same to be a part of our life. As we learn to treat ourselves with respect, we will trust ourselves more. As we allow into our life only others who respect us, we will trust others more.

Of course, as with all components of healing trauma, developing a sense of trust also requires that we address the limiting beliefs we developed because of our threatening environment as children. Using a healing protocol that productively resolves limiting beliefs such as "I can't count on anyone" and "I can't trust myself" can free us from the paralyzing limitations that come with distrust.

Amy was undervalued at her job. She competently handled many aspects of her boss's business in the beauty industry. Her clients loved her and she passionately served them, providing an extra touch of compassion and kindness. I wondered if Amy had considered running her own business, since she seemed to have all the necessary skills and could make a much better living, including no longer being at the whim of her boss.

Amy loved the idea but lacked the confidence to pursue it. We explored the beliefs holding her back. She said, "I don't believe in myself." During our healing work, she recalled that growing up, her parents routinely told her, "You don't want that," "That's not a good choice for you," and even "I know you better than you know you." We cleared these limiting beliefs and provided the healing her inner child needed. After this work, Amy said she felt a significant shift in her ability to be her own boss when the time was right.

Albert Einstein said, "The most important decision we make is whether we believe we live in a friendly or hostile universe." Childhood trauma convinces us that we fundamentally lack safety in the world. To have a full life, however, we must transform limiting beliefs about trust and safety. If we spend our energy trying to control life, we maintain our states of lack, fear, and distrust, which are associated with powerlessness. Although it might not initially be easy to actively create the capacity for more trust in life, it will not happen if we stay passive.

You can slowly and persistently take steps to begin to trust life. Challenge yourself to notice each day how the song on the radio has some helpful wisdom at just the right time, how a phone call from a friend is well timed, or how a podcast, article, or stranger in the grocery store provides information that gives you some relief or a laugh. If you are intentional about creating a sense of safety in life, you will see that over time you can begin to feel much more at ease. Be patient and persistent with this facet of trauma recovery, because cultivating a sense of trust and safety is one of the more complex parts of healing.

Pillar 8

Inner Child Healing

We are multidimensional beings; we are complex, with many parts. One of our many aspects is our wounded inner child, the part of us that did not feel properly loved or safe in childhood. For true healing we must address the unmet needs of our inner wounded child parts and integrate them into our wholeness. This enables us to develop a deeper trust in life and to move through adulthood feeling more complete and empowered.

The wounded inner child represents the fragmented parts of us that dissociated because it was too scary to stay present when we did not feel safe. If we are unable to fight or flee when in danger, and if social engagement is unavailable or ineffective, the default survival response is to freeze. When we freeze, we dissociate, or disconnect, from ourselves. This is a behavior that is meant to prepare us for death so that we do not feel the full impact of the fatal blow. With each scary and unmanageable encounter we have as children, part of us disconnects from our wholeness. The dissociated, or fragmented, parts stay behind, trapped in a time capsule, reliving the horror that led to the need to freeze, while the rest of us grows up. These dissociated parts often do not realize that the traumatic event is over.

Our wounded inner child carries the beliefs of fear and limitation. This is the basis of our ego. During the first seven years of life, we are sponges. Before the emergence of brain development that allows for critical thinking, our subconscious mind records everything we experience without verifying the validity of the data. Painful experiences are categorized as dangerous and are associated with fear, shame, and abandonment. Our ego then uses the information associated with negative experiences to justify its attempt to protect us from pain. This is the part of us that routinely produces an onslaught of negative and fear-based thoughts, encouraging us to avoid risk, stay small, and not believe in ourselves. Healing the wounded inner child allows the ego and its associated fears to be quelled.

Our wounded inner child is the part of us that gets triggered. This is the part that gets upset when life is not fair, when we are not seen or heard, or when we think we are not good enough. Our inner child gets our attention through strong emotional or physical reactions when we are reminded of unresolved trauma. A fight with a dismissive partner, being criticized by a demanding supervisor, and feeling left out of a social event can lead to emotional reactivity from our inner child, who did not feel seen or heard while growing up. Feeling negative emotion or physical pain is often an indicator that our inner child needs our loving attention.

Our well-being is contingent on our ability to respect our inner child. This was undeniable to me after a session with psychologist Willem Lammers. I told him how confused I was about still being seriously limited physically, despite how much I had healed emotionally. I felt free in many ways, but I couldn't even take a brief walk because of the pain and physical exhaustion that followed. In our work together a belief was revealed: "There is hell to pay if I move." I recalled that when I was a young child, no matter what I did, it was wrong, and I could be hurt for every move I made. I constantly felt that emotional or physical violence was imminent, so I was commonly in a freeze state, compelled to survive by being still. With that memory my physical limitations suddenly made sense. As an adult, any time I pushed it by disregarding my need for limited mobility I would have a setback. My inner two-year-old did not make exceptions for experiences like a short vacation, accompanying one daughter for her senior picture photo shoot, or helping my other daughter settle in at college.

In my work, I commonly help clients heal their inner wounded child. We identify a present trigger, which is a request from the inner child to address an unresolved trauma. We use the trigger as a guide, taking us to one of the client's original wounds. I then lead the client through a process of using their adult self to care for their inner child in the way they would love and comfort their own child so they provide the nurturing and validating presence that their inner child has been craving.

Using visualization, these cycle breakers allow their inner child to express through words, movement, or emotion what they were forced to suppress. This allows the inner child to be seen, heard, and respected. Through this inner child healing process the adult self meets their inner child's unmet needs for nurturing and safety. It may mean that the adult part stands up to their childhood abusers, rescues the child self, or gives or does whatever else the child wanted at the time of the trauma but could not have or could not do.

Inner child healing also can include a tour, provided by the adult self, whereby the child is shown how the adult self has made it, thanks to the inner child's will and creativity. The adult shows the inner child the highlights of life, featuring all the good that has been cultivated. This is meant to honor the inner child for coping, which made it possible to become an adult, as well as to let the inner child know that they no longer need to hang on to the past, because it is over, and the adult has "got it" now.

The process of inner child healing also involves identifying and clearing the limiting beliefs that emerged from traumatic experiences. These steps complete the traumatic event and restore empowerment. We then invite the child part to integrate with the adult, allowing for more wholeness.

Addressing the needs of the wounded inner child helps us productively release the pain that caused the child, and therefore the adult, to feel stuck, trapped, powerless, and traumatized. The wounded inner child parts realize through this process that the past is over and it is now safe to come home. Inner child healing work brings tremendous relief from trauma.

Not only does the inner child need healing from past hurts, but how the inner child is treated in the present is crucial as well. We adults must be mindful of how we are treating ourselves in the present to heal our inner child, because our adult self can be the culprit when our inner child is in distress. This means when we criticize ourselves, we criticize our inner child. When we are impatient, we are impatient with our inner child. When we treat ourselves like our abusive parents treated us, by judging, criticizing, invalidating, and punishing ourselves, we are perpetuating the abuse our inner child has already experienced. When we pick up where our parents left off, we are abusing ourselves.

To heal, it is important for us to recognize that our adult self is not separate from our inner child. We are one being, containing both aspects. Though the inner child is holding the pain from childhood, this part of us is also us. Rejecting the inner child who holds resistance, anger, and fear creates an internal division. We cannot feel good and stay disconnected from our inner child. Our inner child demands to be heard. If we ignore the cries for acknowledgment and healing, our inner child will get our attention through body symptoms, emotional reactivity, and other trauma reenactments. The goal is to work with the parts of us that disconnected as a result of trauma, and to heal them and integrate them into our wholeness. When we are operating through the lens of love and compassion, we can recognize when our inner child is crying out, as evidenced by reactions to triggers, and give them what they need to release the pain and limiting beliefs that developed as a result of trauma.

There are many ways to bring healing to your inner child. Some methods are best done with a skilled professional. Until we can truly have love and compassion for our inner child, it's important to have the support of a professional to guide this healing work. When you are ready and able, you can bring healing to your inner child on your own.

For example, Anna grew up in Colorado but had not wanted to go back there as an adult. She experienced emotional abuse and other hardships in her youth. Additionally, the family moved many times, which made school and social belonging difficult. Recently, Anna reluctantly agreed to house-sit for a relative who lived near her hometown. However, she found herself feeling very cranky during her stay, and as she contemplated what was bothering her, she realized her difficult childhood caused some of her inner child parts to be left behind. Deciding to rectify this, she drove to each of the three homes where she had lived and, while sitting in her car in front of the houses, lovingly and playfully retrieved her inner child. She said she later felt much better emotionally, and the rest of her stay in Colorado was pleasant.

Another way to create healing for your inner child is to engage in activities you enjoyed when you were young. What did you love to do when you were a child? When did you feel the safest, the freest, and the happiest? It is my hope that, even if you had the bleakest of childhoods, you had some experiences where you had fun and felt free and playful. Regularly treat yourself and your inner child to these activities. A trip to the park, zoo, or skating rink can create the experiences necessary for allowing your inner child parts to trust you, which can allow the frozen energy associated with the past to be released.

It can also be helpful to ask yourself what you missed out on. Did you long to put a model airplane together with your dad but he was working, drinking, or otherwise unavailable? Did you long for a parent to play catch with you, take you to get your hair done, or take you bowling? When you give yourself what you missed out on, you are being your own hero, comforter, nurturer, supporter, and healer.

Our inner child represents the parts of us that could not tolerate the stress we faced while growing up and that have been longing for safety, validation, acceptance, and love our whole lives. When we love this part of us, we heal. We become the parent our younger self has always wanted. We could not control how our parents treated us, but we can control how we treat ourselves. We come full circle when, as an adult, we can treat our own inner child the way we always wanted to be nurtured and cherished. We become the one we were waiting for.

Pillar 9

Emotional Mastery

One of the most accurate measures of well-being is the ability to regulate our emotional state. This means that when we feel anxious, we can calm ourselves and when we feel depressed, we can lift our own mood. Self-regulation is the ability to experience and metabolize strong emotions, allowing us to move through them instead of suppressing them or acting them out. A tremendous level of freedom is achieved when we can cultivate the ability to tolerate and regulate the whole range of emotional experiences. The person who has learned how to successfully master unpleasant emotions is a superhero, and we all have the possibility of earning our cape.

We are not born knowing how to self-regulate. Infants learn how to do this when parents are well regulated as they interact with them. When upset infants are comforted by parents who are calm, they are soothed. When infants consistently receive nurturing from parents, they learn to comfort themselves over time. Attunement facilitates the capacity for resiliency and effective emotion regulation. This is an enormous gift healthy parents give their children.

Traumatized parents, however, are incapable of teaching their children something they themselves never learned to do. They pass their inability to calm themselves on to their children. These children grow into adults who have a dysregulated nervous system and a poor ability to self-soothe, which is a predominant cause of anxiety, irritability, fear, outbursts of anger, and harming others.

None of us enjoy the feeling states associated with disappointment, anger, sadness, and jealousy, but without them we could not evolve. Emotions are not the enemy: They hold the information we need to transcend our pain. Our emotions represent the thoughts, beliefs, expectations, and perspectives we hold, much of which comes from childhood.

Therefore, our templates from childhood are often the gatekeepers of how we feel emotionally. When we are experiencing unpleasant emotions, the key to emotional freedom is to go within, uncovering the woundedness that is holding us hostage to emotional pain. For example, if you feel rejected because a new acquaintance seems disinterested in a friendly relationship, you may have an emotional reaction because of your childhood template of unworthiness. An exploration of your history can reveal the real reason for your feelings of rejection. For example, perhaps you felt rejected by your parents or others. Healing the original wounds from childhood related to rejection can help you ultimately realize that when someone doesn't want a relationship with you, it's not an indicator of your unworthiness, and you can more easily accept that the relationship simply isn't a good fit. Addressing the unresolved trauma with the prompting of our unpleasant emotions allows us to heal the trauma responsible for our emotional instability.

Difficulties related to emotions also result from suppressing how we feel. When there is limited physical or emotional safety, a child must suppress a vast array of urges, impulses, thoughts, and feelings, which leads to unprocessed emotions. This suppressed information is a storehouse of unhealed pain and serves as a land mine for emotional eruptions when we get triggered.

Emotions tend to lodge in specific areas of the body. For example, fear is often stored in the kidneys, anger is stored in the liver, and concern about lack of support resides in the lower back. These trapped emotions block the flow of energy in the body and can lead to anxiety, depression, difficulty concentrating, chronic pain, and illness. We need to be able to freely express ourselves, and when we cannot, the cost is high for all aspects of our well-being.

Not only do we need to release stored emotions, but it is also important to learn to stop suppressing emotions. Traumatized adults are conditioned to suppress unwanted emotions long after there is a safety reason to do so. Many of us suppress anger because we were trained in childhood to be "good" to avoid getting in trouble. We also suppress anger as adults because we don't want to be like our hostile parents, or because we want others to like us. We suppress other emotions like grief and disappointment because we never learned the value of feeling our feelings; in fact, many people do not know how to effectively do this. As we heal and gain more confidence, we can learn to discard survival strategies such as perfectionism and suppression, enabling us to be more present for life.

Releasing victimhood is another way to gain better emotional regulation. Being a victim can become our identity after childhood trauma, a default reaction that can make us vulnerable to being reactive instead of reflective and empowered.

To release victimhood we must develop awareness of when we are thinking, feeling, and behaving like a victim. In his book *A Game Free Life*, Dr. Stephen Karpman discusses an insightful model referred to as the drama triangle that reveals the various states of disempowerment that lead to emotional suffering. The three roles in this triangle are *rescuer, persecutor,* and *victim.*

Someone in the role of *rescuer* wants to fix an unwanted situation for another person and is more concerned about a quick remedy for discomfort than finding a solution to the bigger issues at hand. The *persecutor* is the person who condemns the victim. The persecutor blames, criticizes, and attempts to manipulate others in order to feel superior and control them. The *victim*, driven by feelings of helplessness and powerlessness, believes someone else is responsible for both their problems and the solutions. Victims can feel sorry for themselves, blame people, and expect others to take care of them. By becoming a rescuer, persecutor, or victim, we create unnecessary suffering for ourselves and others. The anger and resentment in these interactions can turn us into the very people we have resented for hurting us. Learning how to regulate our emotional state can prevent us from participating in the drama triangle.

Our nervous system is constantly using information in our environment to determine how to respond to life. When learning to regulate our emotions, it can be helpful to understand what is meant by the *window of tolerance,* which is the zone of optimal arousal where someone feels more emotional ease and copes well with life. When our stress level is too high, we feel overwhelmed and can become hypervigilant and reactive, or can feel numb, unmotivated, depressed, and empty. When we feel threatened, we can easily fall outside our window of tolerance where we are more likely to participate in the drama triangle.

We can increase our window of tolerance and therefore build the capacity for self-regulation in many ways. First, we can address the underlying unresolved emotional pain that keeps us traumatized. This helps reduce triggers. Second, we need tools, or a plan of action, for when strong emotions are felt.

Here are steps to support yourself when you feel triggered:

- **Step 1.** Be the observer, offering yourself compassion as soon as possible after noticing that you have lost your peace. This requires mindfulness. Strong emotion is a clue that you have been triggered. Accept that you have been triggered and that you feel the way you feel.
- **Step 2.** Feel the emotion in your body. Notice where you feel the sensation of the emotional reaction. Tightness in your gut? Pressure in your chest? Notice the sensations and allow yourself to be present with what you feel physically. Breathe.
- **Step 3.** Put words to what you are experiencing. It can be helpful to say to yourself, or out loud, "I notice I am angry," or "I feel scared, but I am not in danger." It can also help to give yourself permission to feel your emotions. You can tell yourself, "It's okay to feel this."
- **Step 4.** Ask yourself, "What is the story I am telling myself about this situation? What are the thoughts, beliefs, perceptions, or memories associated with my reactivity?"
- **Step 5.** Use a tool to help you work through the activated emotion. Tools can include taking a mindful walk, breathing, using the Emotional Freedom Technique, journaling, self-coaching with Logosynthesis, crying, spending time in nature, listening to music, praying, surrendering, or talking with a supportive person. Whatever tool you choose, remember to feel what you are feeling. Tools help us feel and move through distress, not bypass or distract ourselves from our pain.

I know it can sound counterintuitive to befriend your emotions. To some degree, the success of capitalism is built on keeping you from being in touch with how you really feel; for example, people who want to numb themselves are targets for industries such as drugs, gaming, and liquor. To be free, though, we must learn how to feel. Resistance leads to constriction; feeling leads to freedom.

Give yourself permission to feel your emotions. Imagine your emotions are like butter and you are warm toast: Let them melt into you while you rest and breathe. Once you get past the resistance and can calmly sink into the physical sensations of your emotions, you will begin to relax. This is self-healing. You will find that as you acquire tools for emotional regulation, situations that previously upset you no longer hold a charge. You will feel more confident, knowing that when difficulty arises, you can handle it. Most importantly, you will learn that not only is it safe to feel, but it is also the way to earn your cape.

Befriend Your Body

Our body is in service to our mission. I watched a YouTube video of a dance performance of the Georgia School of Dance and Theater using the song "Stand Up." Moved by their incredible talent, I watched it over and over. These people were connected to their Essence, and the strong, graceful bodies of the dancers were integral to this powerful performance. The words of the director were icing on the cake: "We are more powerful and progressive when we unite and uplift each other. Through common purpose, determination and resilience, we can grow, survive and thrive—as individuals, communities, nations, and as a world." The performance was a service to humanity.

Our physical bodies assist us in achieving what we are here to do. Pain fueled my spiritual awakening. Its intensity made it impossible to say no to the extensive tasks necessary to heal myself. My inability to be physically active for many years kept me at home. Although I longed to but could not go on long hikes, travel, or even go out to dinner with friends, I was given plenty of time to rest, spend time with my husband and daughters, and consume vast amounts of personal growth material. If my physical body had been in alignment with my ambition, I'm not sure I would have had the self-control necessary to avoid being a permanent workaholic or to invest in my well-being in the manner necessary to heal myself. Achieving my purpose required me to have an injured, weak, and fragile body, at least for a period of time. Through the extensive process to restore my physical health, I gained wisdom about the relationship of trauma, health, and healing.

We Are Responsible for Healing Ourselves

It is impossible to experience developmental trauma without it affecting the physical body. Our mind, body, and spirit are inextricably connected, and high levels of stress can severely impact our body. For people with disease, it can seem as though symptoms have come from nowhere, though physical illness is often years in the making. We do not notice the warning signs that we are imbalanced because of disconnection from our body, which happens with trauma. It does not feel safe to be in a body when we are under routine threat.

Early in my trauma recovery, I became aware of the teachings of Louise Hay in which she explained that certain illnesses commonly correspond with specific psychological states. For example, I learned problems with heavy metal toxicity can be associated with poor boundaries, and thyroid issues are connected to the inability to speak up for oneself.

When I began reading about the association between health and psychology, my immediate response was to blame myself for being sick. My conditioning from childhood was "It's my fault," so I assumed the failures of my body were the result of my inadequacy. As my story of trauma unfolded and I learned more about the true cause of most chronic illnesses, I felt relief knowing trauma from my childhood was to blame for my physical limitations and not my inadequacy as a person.

To live an empowered life, regardless of why we are sick, we must take responsibility for our healing. We cannot blame doctors, therapists, or anyone else when we are not making progress. If we are not benefiting from our current treatment, it is up to us to find someone who can effectively help.

Many people in the helping community do not understand the impact of childhood trauma on our physical and emotional health. It is important to accept that not all people in health care are going to offer the appropriate course of treatment for us. Even when working with providers who are trauma-informed, recovery can be multifaceted and complex. If you do not currently have people in your life who support you in healing, please consider that as you align with your Essence and follow its cues, you will have all the help you need.

Our Body Is Doing the Best It Can

It is not unusual for those of us with undesirable physical symptoms to feel at war with our bodies. We can feel frustrated with our body for its aches and pains, digestive dysfunction, limited sexual responsiveness, and lack of physical stamina. We may hate our bodies for being under- or overweight, or for other perceived imperfections in our appearance.

Like most people with a trauma history, I had a complicated relationship with my body. I was angry, impatient, and judgmental of it for how it functioned. There were times I wished for anyone's body but mine. My attitude reflected how I felt about my parents, my inner child, and life itself. I felt betrayed.

If we are disconnected from Essence, we blame our body for "misbehaving" without realizing our symptoms are merely bringing attention to something we critically need to know. To be well, we must accept that our body is not our enemy. It is on our side. It is remarkably resilient and durable despite the symptoms it presents, which may suggest otherwise. We must commit to treating our body with the respect and love it deserves. It is our only vessel in which to experience this life, and we must learn to honor, appreciate, and adore it to be healthy, no matter what.

Emotional Healing Precedes Physical Healing

Your body must feel safe to come out of a chronic fight-or-flight state. The depth of emotional pain we experience, which stems from the sadness, anger, disappointment, and despair of our troubled youth, keeps our body in a holding pattern. Our bodies will not heal if there is a higher priority, because attending to emotional pain and ongoing fear are superior needs. To achieve desirable health, we must first address our emotional backlog. This involves learning to feel and express our emotions, wants, and needs in the present moment and releasing the stored emotions from a difficult childhood. As we feel safer, which happens when we heal our trauma, our body can shift out of survival mode and into healing mode.

Symptoms Are Communication from Our Body

Wellness requires us to listen to the wisdom of our bodies. Every physical symptom holds a key to feeling good. I regularly help my clients identify the messages embedded in their physical symptoms. For example, a headache could be a cue that we are dehydrated. It could also mean we are too much "in our head." A headache can reflect that we have eaten too much sugar or are tolerating disrespect. It can also tell us there is a trauma that needs healing.

Margaret, a client with an extreme amount of trauma from various sources in her childhood, came to therapy one day with a four-day migraine. This seasoned client knew the drill. With my guidance, she focused on the sensory information associated with this migraine. She sensed an image of a clenched fist placed inside her left temple. We used Logosynthesis to address this image, and her migraine instantly turned into a mild headache. We then focused on the message embedded in the headache.

The headache reminded her of the horrific car accident she was in at age sixteen that required the Jaws of Life to extract her. She described watching the aftermath of the accident as though she were a witness. She had dissociated, and this part of her was ready to return; the headache was the entry point. After another round of Logosynthesis, the headache vanished, and she was embraced by an extraordinary sense of peace and increased wholeness as we integrated the part of her that had left because of the trauma. The narcotics she had been taking could neither alleviate nor touch the cause of her pain. Healing requires us to feel what was not felt, to retrieve what has been lost and release what is not ours.

In another example, Cassandra, a client with chronic illness, told me her Crohn's disease symptoms worsened between our sessions. To assist her, I guided her to dialogue with her body, inviting her to tune in to the significance of the sores in her mouth. She realized the sores had appeared after receiving a text from her mom, who had been uncaring throughout her life. In fact, when Cassandra was recovering from cancer her mother was still unable to show compassion. The recent text had triggered resentment, which her body communicated through mouth sores. I invited Cassandra to imagine saying to her mother what she had held in. She visualized telling her mom how she really felt, after which the sores immediately disappeared.

Wellness requires learning to love your body, listening to its cues, and responding accordingly. If our body is tired, we must rest. If we eat toxic food, we must make healthier choices. If our body doesn't feel safe around people with narcissism, we need to avoid them. When we lean into the challenges associated with our body, instead of numbing, avoiding, and projecting, the body and its symptoms can lead us back to who we really are.

We Can Stay Sick Because of Secondary Gain

When we are mistreated as children, we do not get the attention we need, which creates a longing to feel important. The attention from doctors and concerned friends can feel so good to some people that they may not realize a part of them doesn't want to get better, because being unwell may seem like their only way to feel important. This is not something most people intentionally do, nor do they even realize it is happening.

Secondary gain is something worth exploring for those with chronic health concerns. You may want to ask yourself the following questions: "What does my illness allow me to avoid?" "What do my health limitations bring into my life that I otherwise would not have?" "How do my health challenges invite others to meet my unmet needs from childhood?"

Our Relationship with Food Matters

Cultivating a positive association with food improves your relationship with your body. Food is often a challenge for traumatized people, and I was not exempt. During my recovery, I realized I hated food. For years, I ate an extremely clean diet free of processed and other inflammatory foods. Almost everything I ingested was organic and GMO-free and did not come in a box or a package, and definitely not from a restaurant.

However, regardless of how healthfully I ate, my body hurt. I routinely felt awful after I ate any food. As I began to dig deeper into the connection between eating and pain, I recalled an abusive incident from my childhood associated with food. One night my mom served soup for supper. I was hungry and my soup was hot, so I blew on it quite hard. Immediately I felt an excruciating blow to my head and was stunned to realize my dad had hit me hard, irritated with how I was blowing on my soup. As I unpacked this and other abusive incidents associated with food, I realized my brain equated food with danger. My body felt under threat of attack anytime I ate, making it impossible to properly digest food.

Poor food digestion and difficulty digesting life are related. Traumatic experiences can occur in a manner that is too much, too fast, and too soon. Traumatic experiences also result from not being given enough of what we need. Their very nature makes them impossible to metabolize at the time of impact. As we heal trauma and take care of our bodies, the digestive problems related to food often can improve, but it may also be important to work with professionals who understand developmental trauma, nutrition, and working with the whole person to restore a healthy, functioning body.

We Need Support from Professionals
Who Understand Trauma

As we work to heal emotionally and mentally from developmental trauma, the nervous system recovers and the release of tension and stress helps heal the physical body. However, it may also be important to work with trauma-informed professionals to assist in rebalancing the body. In my recovery I worked with a number of energy healers and body workers who used a variety of methods. Each approach met a unique need. I have used acupuncture, chiropractic care, massage, Hellerwork, visceral manipulation, physical therapy, Rolfing, craniosacral therapy, pain neutralization therapy, and MyoKinesthetic therapy, NeurOptimal neurofeedback, and quantum biofeedback.

After many years of enduring extreme abuse, every structure, cell, system, tissue, and organ in my body was affected. These were not things that the physicians I saw for years knew how to detect or treat. I experienced immense relief working with skilled bodyworkers, who put their hands on my body in a nurturing and educated manner, validated my suffering without feeling sorry for me, and worked in partnership with me to heal my body. These people helped my body learn to feel safe in relationships with others.

A gifted bodyworker with a gentle soul, Elaine helped my body release protective defensive patterns that held substantial body tension. With her gifted and wise hands, she helped me coax my internal organs back into place from under my ribs, where they had retreated for safety. Cole guided me on shamanic journeys and helped me relate to my body as a sanctuary. Her open heart provided the safety my body craved. Michelle, a caring pelvic-floor physical therapy specialist with a good sense of humor and a strong intuition about where her hands were needed, helped me release pain, constriction, and fear from my pelvis and abdomen, allowing them to release their death grip. The state of your body represents what you have been through, from how others have treated you to how you have treated yourself. Illness is often a reflection of the accumulation of disrespect from all sources. Poor health comes from an inability to say no to what separates you from your Essence, such as low-vibrational food, people, and environments. It also happens when you agree to please others despite what you really want. Physical vitality hinges upon our commitment to emotional, mental, and spiritual wellness.

Can you consider befriending your body? Can you entertain the notion that your body is always in service to you? You can't heal your body all at once, but can you be 10 percent nicer to your body today? And tomorrow? As you remove the barriers to deeply loving yourself, you will eventually see how your body is in service to you despite how you feel. And when you give love back to your body, which it innately has for you, your symptoms will soften. Maybe they will even disappear.

Pillar II

Love

L ove is the absence of separation. It is the certainty that we are not separated from the Divine, from one another, or from all of creation. Love dissolves negativity. It is absent of judgment of self and others, absent of distrust and worry. Love is knowing that I am you and you are me.

Accessing the power of our heart is how we love. Our higher self communicates with us through our heart, and when we are attuned to the wisdom of this genius, we can more easily navigate life, knowing that we are Divine beings. We learn that people who trigger us are merely a reflection of ourselves, and we learn to thank them for what they evoke in us, because exposure to the wound provides an opportunity to heal.

Why is it hard to love? Why is it difficult to open our hearts even when we want to? In part our time on Earth is meant to test our ability to navigate the perception of separateness through various manifestations of hardship, including childhood trauma. We are faced with the illusion of separateness with job loss, conflict with others, the consequences of natural disasters, and any other unwanted experience that provokes the possibility of resistance to life. When we encounter suffering, we often question why a challenge is happening to us. We may blame others and feel resentment. This resistance naturally leads us to self-protect, to shield ourselves from more pain. The part of us that largely takes the brunt of this shutdown is our heart.

How do we more fully access the wisdom of our heart and our capacity to love? The great mystic poet Rumi said, "Your task is not to seek for love, but merely to seek and find all the barriers within yourself that you have built against it." The tenderness of our heart is what allows us to love so deeply and is why we feel so much pain. Our natural response when we are hurting is to protect ourselves with varying levels of armor, depending on the depth of pain we have experienced. This armor is a requirement for children who endure suffering at the hands of parents and had to shield their hearts from unbearable pain. As we heal one layer at a time, we address that which was meant to protect us but now makes us numb and guarded and lack empathy.

Children who experience developmental trauma can begin to loathe themselves before they even have language. The template of self-hatred emerges from experiences of rejection and abandonment from parents who are critical or negligent, leaving children to think they are the problem. Beliefs emerge, including "I am a burden," "I am not enough," "I am too much," and "I am unlovable." We also inherit self-condemning beliefs from our parents, who grew up feeling the same way. Adding to the template of unworthiness are other experiences, including being criticized by teachers, peers, coaches, and others, which further fuels a negative self-perception, separating us even more from knowing love. The accumulation of heartache diminishes the possibility we can love ourselves or anyone else.

What complicates feelings of self-criticism is that our judgment of self can begin at a very young age and deepen over time, making us completely unaware of why we don't like ourselves. Thus, low self-worth feels normal, as if it is who we are and not the result of something that happened to us. I often hear wounded people say, "I cannot believe I did that,"

"I am so stupid," "I am so mad at myself for [fill in the blank]," and "How could I have done that?" These types of responses become automatic; we are often not aware we are harming ourselves with our thoughts and words. This is self-abuse.

In addition to childhood programming that convinces us we are not worth loving, lack of self-forgiveness limits our capacity for love. When we have been unable to forgive ourselves for what are essentially complications stemming from trauma, we disconnect further from our Essence, and so from love. This can happen in a variety of ways.

Before healing from trauma we can hurt ourselves with self-destructive and impulsive behaviors such as socializing with judgmental people, taking jobs in demeaning environments, and neglecting and abusing our bodies. We can engage in addictive behaviors, inflicting more pain on ourselves with forms of self-harm like excessive and dangerous drug use, sex, and gambling. We then judge and shame ourselves for these behaviors.

We also struggle to forgive ourselves for hurting others. Difficulty with self-regulation can lead to impatience and irritability with, or even abuse of, others. Causing harm to others can exacerbate feelings of shame and regret, adding to the vicious attacks we often already launch toward ourselves.

Holding victim energy as a result of our unhealed pain and loss of personal power can make us targets for other wounded people. When we have not yet healed, we can continue to be victimized. Difficulty setting boundaries, self-sacrifice, and people-pleasing behavior may allow others to exploit us. We may then feel angry and disappointed with ourselves.

We may also struggle to forgive ourselves for feeling anger, resentment, and bitterness toward people who hurt us. It is natural to experience these reactions, but when we hang on to resentment too long, we further wound ourselves.

Finally, it is important to forgive ourselves for choosing to experience the pain we have been through. Our spirit elected this life before our personality was formed. Thus, we experience in physical form the fluid plan our soul laid out for us. Our humanness can't fully grasp the complexity of why we experience what we do. To use a metaphor, if there is an insect in your house and you don't want to kill it, you can slide paper underneath it to transport it outdoors. The bug will be alarmed and panicked, terrified and confused. It can't know that, even though it is scared and uncomfortable, we are doing what is best for it.

How do you learn to love yourself after a lifetime of being convinced there is something fundamentally wrong with you? How do you forgive yourself for the pain you have caused yourself and others? You start by deciding that you want to. No one can do it for you, and it requires consistent dedication to heal your original wounds and the negative beliefs you hold about yourself, life, and others.

Recovery from trauma asks us to put ourselves first. This can be a challenge for adults who were conditioned as children to believe their needs did not matter or were taught that self-care is selfish. For adults who are used to prioritizing the needs of others, to avoid rejection or punishment, putting themselves first can be a radical idea.

Self-care involves many daily decisions where we choose to give ourselves what we need and want. This includes making mindful decisions about who we spend time with and what we spend our time doing and not doing. Self-care is getting enough rest, setting boundaries, and doing things we enjoy. It is the gentle and compassionate way we talk to ourselves. It is learning to be amused with our quirkiness and imperfections. Self-care originates from a willingness to love ourselves.

Masaru Emoto, author of many books including *The Hidden Messages in Water* and *Love Thyself: The Message from Water III*, was a water pioneer and a kindness teacher. He conducted experiments on water to demonstrate the power of our thoughts, words, music, and prayer on its molecular structure. He labeled small containers of water with a variety of words and froze them. He then looked at the frozen water crystals under a microscope and photographed them. The results showed that the structure of the crystals varied, depending on how the water container had been labeled. Positive words of love and kindness produced beautiful water crystals, and words associated with hate and negativity led to displeasing and even disturbing images within the water crystals. His work is compelling evidence of the importance of kindness. Most of our body is composed of water. Perhaps Emoto's work can inspire you to be mindful of how you talk to yourself, knowing your water molecules are listening.

Love is an empowering priority to make in our life. Treating ourselves with kindness, respect, and love changes everything. People are nicer, life is smoother, and we are happier.

One day at work I was feeling especially full of love for myself. I was walking down the hall in my office building when a woman I had never seen before stopped me and said, "You look amazing!" I smiled and thanked her. She went on, "I'm not kidding—you look really, really, good!" I laughed to myself because I knew without a doubt this was life reflecting to me the love I felt for myself. This experience marked a milestone in my own personal growth. I had felt self-hatred for many years, but not anymore. If I can turn it around, you can, too.

It is encouraging that there is currently a self-love revolution. It's becoming popular to love yourself. More than ever before, people feel they have permission to take care of themselves, to surrender self-sacrifice as a badge of honor, and to set boundaries. People are waking up and aspiring to elevate their sense of self-worth. We are moving beyond the perception that getting our nails done and going on a shopping spree are the ideals of self-care. People are journaling, take personal growth courses, and joining communities of like-minded people who aspire to be empowered. The next step beyond a self-love revolution is simply a love revolution. What we have yet to realize as a civilization is that there is no "other." Therefore, there is no separation between self-love and love for others. There is only love.

Pillar 12

Thought Mastery

One delicate topic related to personal growth for trauma survivors is the matter of mindset. There is a movement in society to "be positive." Although this may appear as progress from people's tendency to complain and criticize, it can be a hidden form of gaslighting.

Trauma creates deeply entrenched patterns of fear and negativity that demand we focus on lack and limitation as a survival strategy. Beliefs developed in childhood such as "My life is so hard," "Nobody likes me," and "Nothing goes my way" are the guiding force behind many thought patterns for wounded adults.

This negativity is fueled by hurt, fear, and the need to self-protect. People recovering from developmental trauma are in a lot of pain. Emotional flashbacks, feeling rejected, isolated, and sad, and physical pain are difficult experiences. There is no way to sidestep dealing with the emotional consequences of childhood trauma. Pain of all kinds must be faced and felt.

When traumatized people are told to look on the bright side in the various ways our society advocates positivity, a trauma reenactment can occur, where the positivity promoter mimics the behavior of parents who could not see or hear us. Toxic positivity, as it is known, can evoke feelings of abandonment.

The challenge for a cycle breaker is learning to navigate both the need to process trauma, which includes managing powerful surges of emotions like desperation and despair, and cultivating a mindset that keeps moving us forward. There is tremendous value in an optimistic attitude, but not at the expense of dismissing our pain. The formula for managing this dichotomy is first to let ourselves feel what we feel. This may look like crying, wailing, cursing, sobbing, and other forms of emotional expression when we get hit with trauma triggers. Dealing with our pain may also include meditating, taking a walk, or writing down how we feel. Only after we have expressed and released what has surfaced can we courageously move forward and focus on possibility.

Why is mindset important? Our thoughts and beliefs create our reality. What we put our attention on expands. When our energy frequency is low, as indicated by depression, frustration, anxiety, or irritability, we draw experiences to us that resonate at the same vibration. Being in a bad mood may lead to conflict with loved ones, getting a flat tire, or stubbing our toe. Focusing on pain can make us feel even worse, and thoughts of material lack can lead to even more financial hardship.

The end of my first pregnancy was stressful. There was a great deal of uncertainty as I was seeking an internship, finishing my dissertation, and planning a move, which required both buying and selling a house. I had a lot of fear associated with these transitions.

During this time, my husband and I were offered a free hotel stay in Branson, Missouri, in return for touring a time-share vacation home. We did not have a good time. We got a speeding ticket on the way, our hotel was old and primitive, and our entire trip felt like one hardship after another. I knew nothing about mindset back then, but now it's easy to see how our negativity was the catalyst for more negativity.

Science explains how our focus draws experiences to us. The reticular activating system (RAS) is the part of our brain that sifts through the enormous amount of data we encounter at any given time. It is impossible for the brain to attend to all incoming and internal data instantaneously, so it filters through information and prioritizes its focus based on where our attention is primarily held.

Have you noticed that once you buy a car, you suddenly see your model everywhere? Or after you name your child, you suddenly become aware of many other children with the same name? These experiences are emotionally charged events that get the brain's attention; the brain then ranks them high in the hierarchy of the RAS.

This is one way that circumstances are brought into our life. Experiences that seem important to us by virtue of how much attention we place on them are drawn to us by the power of our mind. My husband and I were focused on lack and limitation at the time of our trip to Branson; therefore, we experienced even more lack and limitation. We were the creators of the speeding ticket and other unwanted experiences on the trip.

When we focus intentionally on shifting our thoughts, our beliefs can change, which then reflects improvement in our life experience. I listened to Oprah Winfrey talk about overcoming fatigue while on the set of the movie *The Color Purple*. She was quite tired, but her workday was not nearly over. To boost her energy, she started chanting to herself, "I am getting my second wind. I am getting my second wind." She told herself this until it was true.

Shortly after I listened to her story, my acupuncturist suggested I eat a breakfast of bone broth and quinoa each morning to support my health. It tasted awful. I decided to use Oprah's technique to see if it would help me eat this unsavory meal. As I ate, I told myself over and over, "This tastes wonderful! This is so good!" I truthfully did not expect it to work, but I was pleasantly surprised at how much easier it was to tolerate this meal by changing my mindset. I shifted my thoughts, which changed my beliefs, and the result was a more satisfying breakfast.

Dr. Joe Dispenza, a leading expert on mindset, healed himself from a spinal injury using only his mind. In his book *Breaking the Habit of Being Yourself*, he writes about the connection between our thoughts and feelings:

> As you think different thoughts, your brain circuits fire in corresponding sequences, patterns, and combinations, which then produce levels of mind equal to those thoughts. Once these specific networks of neurons are activated, the brain produces specific chemicals with the exact signature to match those thoughts so that you can feel the way you were just thinking. Therefore, when you have great thoughts or loving thoughts or joyous thoughts, you produce chemicals that make you feel great or loving or joyful. The same holds true if you have negative, fearful, or impatient thoughts. In a matter of seconds, you begin to feel negative or anxious or impatient. (p. 57)

Knowing the power of our thoughts can encourage us to take charge of our lives by taking charge of how we think. Byron Katie is well known for her teachings known as "The Work." Her process guides us to mindfully evaluate our thoughts by answering four questions when something upsets us: Is it true? Can you absolutely know that it's true? How do you react, what happens, when you believe that thought? Who would you be without that thought?

I once thought I had a concussion. My beloved hammock fell to the ground while I was in it. My body was sore for a few days and then a headache emerged. I had the idea the pain in my head must be a concussion. I immediately developed a narrative around this, reaching out to various healers and asking for support with my "concussion."

Monika, my real-life spirit guide, challenged me. She wondered if I had seen a doctor. I had not. She suggested I either see a doctor for a diagnosis or question my own belief. I knew she was right. I didn't have many other symptoms of a concussion. What was happening? I was finishing my book and realized my mind was sabotaging me. If I pursued the idea of a concussion, I could be distracted from my book and be sick for a long time. Borrowing Byron's questions, I contemplated: Was it true I had a concussion? I couldn't be certain that I did. Was I absolutely sure it was true I had a concussion? No. How did I react, or what happened, when I believed that thought? Fear, and seeking lots of validation and attention from others. Who would I be without that thought? I would trust that I would feel better soon.

I also became curious about other reasons the idea of a concussion sidetracked me. Was this a trauma reenactment? As I rested and tuned into what I was feeling, a memory surfaced of being in elementary school with a terrible headache and wanting to come home from school, but my mom wouldn't let me. I remember sobbing, being in so much pain and feeling all alone. Maybe the accident happened to promote a healing opportunity. Not one to waste my pain, I worked to resolve the limiting belief "I'm in pain and no one will help me" and felt better.

Another method of thought exploration is a practice called *morning pages*. This technique was developed by Julia Cameron, author of *The Artist's Way*. Her method of self-exploration involves writing three pages of stream-of-consciousness writing as soon as we wake up. The powerful daily practice encourages us to write whatever is on our mind, and it is not meant to be shared. Our thoughts, feelings, ideas, perceptions, fears, and anything else can appear before us on the pages, allowing us to gain clarity and perspective and to let things go.

Buddha said, "All that we are is the result of what we have thought. The mind is everything. What we think we become." Our thoughts can make us suffer or bring us joy. Unless we intentionally identify our thoughts and release what is causing the destructive ones, we will suffer. To really know what is on our mind we must self-reflect. This requires solitude, contemplation, and a commitment to self-exploration. Please know that although it can take tremendous discipline and persistence, the value of examining our thoughts cannot be underestimated. A practice of disciplining our mind is truly a necessary and thoughtful tool for living a meaningful life.

Gratitude

Being in a state of gratitude is a true hallmark of well-being. When we can easily notice what is going well, acknowledge the blessings in our lives, and feel sincerely thankful for the good, life flows with ease and joy. It is not surprising, however, that gratitude, like positivity, is tricky for traumatized people.

When I was still deeply wounded I heard a spiritual teacher explain to a depressed person that she should be grateful because at least she had her breath. I thought, *I wouldn't mind so terribly if I didn't have my breath.* When we are in pain from a traumatic childhood, despair can substantially reduce our capacity for gratitude. By numbing ourselves to prevent feeling overwhelming emotional pain, we also block ourselves from good feelings.

Because of societal pressure to be grateful, many of us feel ashamed of our negativity. We ask ourselves, *Why am I so ungrateful? My life could be worse.* This is self-gaslighting, the practice of minimizing and dismissing our own reality, which we learn to do because it was first done to us. We can also struggle with gratitude because we feel the ratio of positive to negative experiences in life is vastly out of balance, and the good things that do happen can feel like bread crumbs when we want a whole slice.

Early in my healing process I bought a gratitude journal. Day after day I tried to list everything that I could be grateful for, but I felt nothing. I did not get the peace I was told would emerge with this practice. I didn't understand why I didn't feel better. I now know I was incapable of feeling authentic in my gratitude. I meant well and wanted to be grateful, but I was too numb and sad. My armor of pain made gratitude inaccessible. As I healed, gratitude emerged naturally and abundantly.

We cannot fake gratitude. Like everything else, gratitude is an energetic expression. We create a vibration with our words and thoughts. When our words do not match our internal state, there is an energetic misalignment. If someone thanks us for a gift we gave them, we can typically detect their degree of sincerity. On some level, we also know when we are insincere. When we are trying to be grateful but don't mean it, incongruous words and thoughts put us out of integrity with ourselves.

Sincerity requires coherence with our words and thoughts. To create coherence, we begin by focusing on something we do sincerely appreciate. We can remember a kind word, a person who cared, a puppy's snuggle, or the warmth of sunshine. We can even imagine a movie or book character who evokes a positive feeling. This can elevate our mood and connect us to the energy of gratitude. Once we have tapped into feeling appreciation, we can capitalize on the momentum. In this higher vibrational state, we may then be able to acknowledge the good in our lives with sincerity.

One simple step we can take to gently increase our capacity for gratitude is listening to guided gratitude meditations. Led by soothing music and a gentle voice, we can be comforted into a state of relaxation that helps release the tension and resistance that previously interfered with gratitude. Another tactic is to recognize what we have taken for granted when we encounter unexpected difficulties such as a broken dishwasher, a day care that is unexpectedly closed, or other hassle. When we must go without something we took for granted, it can be a reminder to appreciate the small things. Gratitude can also be more easily cultivated when we learn about the hardships of others, such as a friend's serious illness, the death of a loved one, or a house fire that destroyed everything.

Feeling gratitude can enhance our ability to be the intentional creator of our lives. In his book *Becoming Supernatural*, Dr. Joe Dispenza says:

> Gratitude is a powerful emotion to use for manifesting because normally we feel gratitude after we receive something. So the emotional signature of gratitude means it has already happened. When you are thankful or you feel appreciation, you are in the ultimate state to receive. When you embrace gratitude, your body as the unconscious mind will begin to believe it is in that future reality in the present moment. (p. 82)

We experience more ease and contentment when we develop the ability to see the good in our lives. A state of gratitude makes our lives exponentially better. When we can condition ourselves to focus on what is working rather than on what is not, we discard our addiction to pain and suffering and replace it with ease, appreciation, and joy. It takes time, but persistent recognition of the silver linings in your life will help you cultivate a grateful heart. I encourage you to incrementally increase your capacity to see the good in your life and to have gratitude for the pleasure it brings.

Master Your Triggers

One of the most frequent questions I hear is "What can I do when I'm triggered?" It excites me, because it tells me the person is ready to stop suppressing how they feel. Perhaps the numbing tools they previously used are losing their effectiveness, or they want to feel good and are ready to remove the barriers to a happy life. Whatever the motivator, learning to address triggers when they arise is empowering work.

As a reminder, triggers occur because unhealed pain from the past gets activated by a present-time stressor. We know we are triggered anytime we are upset, whether it is anger, guilt, disappointment, shame, or fear. It happens often throughout the day, reflected in things like being irritated because our child did not thank us for the lovely supper we made or feeling rejected because our date two nights ago did not respond to our text.

Typically, what we think is responsible for our distress isn't what we are primarily upset about. When we allow the trigger to be our teacher, we can discover the unhealed pain from the past that has surfaced for healing.

Perhaps we feel angry because our partner did not clean up the kitchen after promising to do so. We may feel justified in our reaction, but if we dig deeper, we could find we were raised by parents who repeatedly failed to keep their promises.

Maybe we felt rejected and inadequate because our boss seemed unimpressed with a project we poured our heart into. However, the original source of our pain could be associated with feeling invisible, dismissed, and ignored by our parents. Our boss simply offered the catalyst for activating our trauma narrative of inadequacy.

Or perhaps we had our heart set on rocky road ice cream but the person ahead of us got the last scoop and we're more devastated than the situation typically would warrant. Again, the real culprit could be deprivation related to growing up poor or times when our parents fell short in meeting our needs.

Situations like these can generate a strong reaction in a traumatized person because they are merely shining a light on an unhealed trauma. We are triggered because the pain related to our original hurts has not been fully processed.

Part of what is painful about triggers is how they are connected to our limiting beliefs. They provide clues to the trauma-related beliefs that perpetuate our trauma and cause us suffering. Using triggers to identify hidden beliefs can be very valuable. Here are examples:

- Elizabeth experienced chronic depression. She restricted her anticipation of anything positive in life and regularly sabotaged herself from experiencing success and happiness. When she had extra money, she commonly incurred an unexpected expense that depleted her nest egg. As we explored the pattern she was unconsciously replicating from childhood with her depression, sabotage, and financial lack, she realized that when she was a child, her mother did not want her to be happy. If something good happened, her mother would criticize her and deflate her self-worth. It literally felt unsafe for her to be happy as a child. The belief cultivated by this impossible dilemma was "If I stay miserable, nothing bad will happen."

- Jack told me about a supervisor at work who bullied him by being highly critical and making inappropriate comments about his mental health. This supervisor gossiped about other coworkers and otherwise seemed unqualified for his job. As bad as that felt, Jack said what was worse was that the other supervisor who witnessed this abuse did nothing. As we explored how this experience reflected a childhood pattern, Jack realized he remembered that his mother emotionally abused him as his father stood idly by. The beliefs associated with this pattern included "No one can help me," "I am powerless," "I don't matter," and "No one cares."

- Eliza felt insecure in her marriage. Because of health challenges she felt inadequate to contribute to household tasks. She said, "How could he love me if I don't get things done?" It was a surprising statement, given how patient and supportive her husband had been throughout her illness. When we explored what was underneath her feelings of insecurity and inadequacy, she recognized that her worth as a child was tied to what she accomplished. The ensuing belief was "My worthiness comes from my accomplishments."

It may seem like a lot of work to reflect on triggers and their meaning, but the alternative is to spend our energy managing feelings of anxiety and depression, fighting with our partner, or feeling irritated with our children. We do not heal if we do nothing. Time does not mend our wounds. We only marinate in our pain and share it with others. When we are triggered, we have a choice: repeat patterns from childhood or face the difficulty and heal our trauma.

When I was in labor with my second daughter, a friend came to support me and my husband in the delivery room. Arriving just as I experienced a painful contraction, she said, "Mindi, we don't know how many contractions it's going to take to deliver this baby, but you do not have to have that contraction again." Her statement softened my distress and allowed me to focus on one contraction at a time, knowing with each one that passed that I was closer to meeting my beloved daughter.

Labor can be a helpful metaphor for healing trauma. When trauma gets activated by an experience in present time, it is like a contraction. It can be painful and intense but is a necessary element of healing. Because emotions were suppressed in childhood, they must now be experienced to be released. Learning to be mindful and present with emotions when triggered brings us one step closer to healing trauma. If we continue to suppress how we feel, we will be repeatedly triggered

It can be uncanny how childhood patterns get replicated in adult life. This happens with people and with our pets. Our gentle and loving dog, Katie, a Cavalier King Charles Spaniel, has been my mirror. My family will tell you that for a long time she really got on my nerves. At one point, she would come and sit next to me and stare at me, as though begging for attention. I would try to give her some affection, but I just wanted her to go away. My life coach helped me to see that Katie was representing me as a child, and I was representing my mom. Just like my mom saw me as a burden she did not want to give any attention to, I felt the same about our dog. This was a trauma reenactment. Life was working through our dog, to show me what needed to be healed.

Another example of a Katie trigger was my perception that she was always in my way when I was in the kitchen. No one else was bothered by this behavior. I eventually realized that how I felt about Katie was how I felt about my inner child: I just wanted her to get out of my way so I could get on with my life.

I was tired of being slowed down by trauma. If I had ignored these dog-generated triggers, I would not have had the insight to do healing work around the specific pattern of neglect I experienced from my mom, and I would not have taken the initiative to slow down and be kinder to my inner child.

When you are triggered, here are some questions to help you do your own detective work to discover the unhealed wounds that are responsible for your reactions:

- What is really bothering me about this situation?
- What is my reaction? How do I feel?
- What does this scenario remind me of from the past?
- Is the triggering person (or pet) showing me something I don't want to see about myself?

Please consider reevaluating your perception of triggers. It is not fun to be triggered, but we don't have to like triggers to use them for growth. When you are reactive, can you begin to acknowledge that the thing upsetting you is simply a trauma reminder? Can you hold yourself with compassion for the pain associated with triggers? Will you allow yourself to get curious about what a trigger is showing you? I promise this gets easier with practice and you will feel empowered as you courageously move toward your triggers rather than retreating from them.

Pillar 15

Forgiveness

I have spent many years considering, contemplating, attempting, striving, and willing myself to forgive. Early in my recovery, deciding to forgive my family as soon as possible appealed to me. I knew much of my suffering was tied up in my hatred toward them. I wanted the most direct route to well-being, so I believed at one point that releasing my anguish could be simply and swiftly achieved with forgiveness. The problem with this plan is that it was not possible. It was spiritual bypassing, which is the process of using a spiritual idea to avoid dealing with the underlying pain.

My very seasoned, gifted, and compassionate therapist, Jim, who I know wanted to tell me what I wanted to hear about the possibility of fast forgiveness, carefully told me it was extremely unlikely to work in the way I had hoped. He taught me that forgiveness happens in layers, over time, not immediately. I tried to be the exception to this rule, but I could not.

Forgiveness means we let go of the need for our perpetrators to confess their mistakes, apologize, or somehow own up to what they did to hurt us. Forgiveness means accepting that what is done is done and withdrawing the energy we were investing in anger and resentment and reinvesting it in creating a good life. Forgiveness is a not a simple decision. It is a complex endeavor requiring a tremendous amount of healing.

When you fully forgive, it is a complete mind, body, and spirit experience, and the feeling is authentic peace.

Many people have experienced shame for lacking forgiveness. After sharing their story of immense suffering with other professionals or clergy, clients have told me that they were advised to "just forgive." This gross invalidation only served to heighten the self-abuse they already experienced. If someone is unable to forgive another person, it is because there is still too much pain.

As Jim taught me, addressing unresolved pain layer by layer is the most effective means toward forgiveness. Healing trauma lets us remove the barriers to forgiveness, which allows us to let go of resentments, and for acceptance and peace to emerge. Ann, a spiritual teacher and healer, brought to my attention the suppressed childhood anger that blocked my capacity to forgive. With her support, I used a variety of methods to help me release suppressed anger, including hypnotherapy, inner child work, guided meditations, writing and burning angry letters, and taking a bat to a strategically placed punching bag in our garage.

Amy helped me release the foreign energy in my body and energy field, including the energy of my abusers, that blocked me from being me and caused me to hang on to my pain. Monika helped me understand how intergenerational abuse in my ancestry led to my own abuse, helping me to heal both myself and my ancestors. These healers helped me gain awareness of how abuse affected my emotional, mental, and behavioral patterns and to change them. Jim, Caroline, Karen, and Damian, all masters at energy work, helped me in their own unique way. I was also fortunate to work with Willem Lammers, the originator of Logosynthesis, and with other caring Logosynthesis practitioners.

My pain was so vast and deep, I required an assortment of professionals to help me, though this may not be necessary for everyone. The support of all these talented professionals enabled me to move toward forgiveness, one step at a time. As I progressed in my healing, I got less angry and less sad and gained more understanding and acceptance. This was my pathway to forgiveness. As Willem Lammers says in *Minute Miracles*, "Forgiveness is not something one does, it is the automatic result of the realization that an alternative was not available at the time" (p. 43).

Forgiveness also naturally unfolds as we realize we chose our life. Although our choices may not have been conscious and intentional from our personality self, some part of us was involved in the creation of our story. The empowerment embedded in taking total responsibility for our lives frees us from feeling victimized. When we can fully stop blaming others and can forgive ourselves for the misperception that we were responsible for our abuse, we are in our power, connected to our Essence, and free.

I now aspire to embody love and therefore embrace forgiveness more and more all the time. I daily work to address the barriers that keep me from being free from the pain of my childhood. I consistently work to understand that everything in my life has happened in Divine order. I do my best to look at all people and situations through the lens of love. I strive to see others who hurt people as the product of generations of pain. When I feel triggered, I work to identify and heal the original wounds and beliefs responsible for my reaction. I work to honor where I am, to accept what I can, and to persistently and lovingly continue to move forward in my life.

Consider your thoughts and beliefs about forgiveness. What are your barriers? I encourage you to contemplate, question, and seek your own wisdom and understanding about what forgiveness means to you. Perhaps like me, your beliefs about forgiveness will evolve as you do.

Pillar 16

Use Your Gifts

I love reading memoirs and watching inspiring documentaries and movies based on true events. I'm inspired by and often feel giddy about the stories of others who have courageously dealt with incredible difficulty. Their stories show that the human spirit is remarkably capable of transcending suffering. People who have triumphed show us it is possible to achieve not only recovery but post-traumatic growth, to ascend to great heights and to make extraordinary contributions to the world.

Amy Purdy was nineteen when her legs were amputated below her knees because of meningitis. She also lost a kidney and her spleen. Sidelined but undeterred as she healed, she continued snowboarding, winning medals in consecutive Paralympics. She was runner-up on *Dancing with the Stars*, competed on *The Amazing Race*, and founded her own organization, Adaptive Action Sports, where she supports disabled athletes who want to compete. Though Amy has experienced enormous hardship, she has also experienced incredible highs by transcending tragedy.

The movie *Indian Horse* is based on a novel by Richard Wagamese about Saul Indian Horse, who suffers the deaths of beloved family members and abandonment by his parents and is placed in a Catholic residential school in the late 1950s. This environment is immensely abusive. The despair felt by some of the children in this oppressive environment leads to their suicides.

Saul's only salvation is the introduction of hockey at the school by a young priest. Saul becomes a very gifted player, which helps him get out of the school and into the home of a loving family in the community. Sadly, his traumatic past sabotages the success he is capable of, and he turns to alcohol to numb his unbearable pain. Nevertheless, Saul ultimately chooses life and embarks on the journey to heal himself. In courageously telling his story he helps to shine a light on the atrocious treatment of Native children.

Megan Phelps-Roper wrote the book *Unfollow* based on her experiences growing up as the granddaughter of Fred Phelps, who was known for picketing at the funerals of soldiers and for carrying graphic and hateful signs protesting homosexuality. Megan's extraordinary memoir tells of being raised in this notorious family and how she realized as a young adult that she did not believe what they believed. As young adults, Megan and her sister Grace abruptly left the family with few resources, and yet all their needs were met. Her story shows how life provides what we need when we align with our Essence. Megan's capacity to both love and forgive her family and herself is inspiring. Once a spokesperson for hate, Megan is now a catalyst for love.

Some people with stories of triumph had loving parents who gave them a solid foundation of confidence, enabling them to more easily tackle hardship. Others, such as Tara Westover, author of *Educated*, had unusually challenging childhoods without significant support from caring adults. As I read memoirs of well-loved people who experienced tragedy later in life, I often felt grief from my own absence of love during childhood. I felt envious of these triumphant people who seemed to be closer to their finish line than I was.

In my own personal growth work I was guided to see that the conditions of my childhood were chosen by my soul before my birth, because they were necessary to prepare me to succeed in achieving my mission. We each have a unique contribution to make. It isn't helpful to compare and judge our circumstances with someone else's. Although it's understandable, it keeps us feeling victimized.

The final stage of the transformational journey, **Completion**, is to take what we have learned and use it to help humanity. The wisdom, insights, creativity, talents, and gifts we have developed as a result of aligning with our Essence are birthed into the world in a manner that suits *our* mission. We are rewarded for our tenacity by feeling good and by having opportunities to share what we learned. We become empowered, happy, and capable, with a deep appreciation for life. Through how we live our lives, we demonstrate to others that returning to our true selves is worth whatever it takes.

Conclusion

Kintsugi is a Japanese art form in which broken pottery is mended with powdered gold, silver, or platinum. It is like the wabi-sabi concept of embracing the imperfect. Rather than discard damaged pottery or fix breaks in a way that disguises imperfections, the practice of kintsugi repairs the broken pottery in a way that illuminates the breakage, making it even more beautiful than the original piece.

Leonard Cohen's song "Anthem" has a notable sentiment: "There is a crack, a crack in everything. That's how the light gets in." I have spent so much of my life trying to conceal my imperfections. I didn't want anyone to see how vulnerable and scared I felt. It didn't feel safe to reveal to others the incredible weakness I felt inside.

Then, I began noticing how our society embraced people like Brené Brown, Lizzo, and Kelly Clarkson, strong, vocal women who were admired for being themselves. These women gave us permission to be real. They made "real" look cool. Their blends of humor and vulnerability helped ignite a chain reaction, and others began dismantling the need to portray perfection as the ideal.

They are part of a movement to claim who we are. The stigma associated with having problems is slowly dissolving, allowing us to be more honest with ourselves and others. People are beginning to publicly acknowledge their tendency to be codependent, anxious, insecure, or depressed. Men and women are pursuing personal growth in increasing numbers. This is good. Acknowledging our pain and limitations helps us access our humanity and appreciate the humanity of others. We are not robots; it hurts when people criticize, demean, and neglect us. When we can acknowledge our wounds in an empowered manner, we make way for the light to come in.

Give yourself permission to heal, grow, and experience life for yourself. If you spent your childhood accommodating the needs of others, you did not learn how to give to yourself. It's time.

Cycle breakers, let's embrace who we are. It's time to rise and shine. Let's come out of hiding. Let's celebrate the beauty emanating from our fractures.

There is safety in numbers. Let's share our stories of heartache and transcendence. Find your community, and practice giving and receiving with like-minded people who see and hear you. You will find that you are not alone and that many people do know how you feel. Your experiences will resonate with others, helping them to also feel less alone. Allowing perpetrators to hold power over us has run its course.

Embrace your story: It's the one you came here to experience.

Appendix

Approaches to Trauma Treatment

Dyadic Developmental Psychotherapy was created by Daniel Hughes, PhD. This approach is very successful at helping relationally traumatized children resolve trauma and develop the capacity for safety within a family and trust in life. In this approach the practitioner and parents relate to a child from the acronym of PACE (playfulness, acceptance, curiosity, and empathy). **Danielhughes.org**

Emotional Freedom Technique (EFT) is a mind-body approach to clearing emotional and physical pain. By tapping on specific meridian points while you focus on your concern, such as anxiety or a pain condition, your brain calms down and your symptoms can improve. **Thetappingsolution.com**

Eye Movement Desensitization and Reprocessing (EMDR) was developed by Francine Shapiro, PhD, as a method to resolve the stress associated with traumatic experiences. As the client focuses on the distressing memory, bilateral stimulation is applied (with sound, lights, or tapping). This process engages the client's internal adaptive information processing capabilities, which can lead to resolving disturbing memories. **Emdr.com**

Logosynthesis was introduced by Willem Lammers, PhD, in 2006 as a simple comprehensive approach for personal growth. It is used in coaching and therapy and for self-healing. The goal is to assist a person in reconnecting with their Essence by restoring the flow of energy required for wholeness. **Logosyntheis.net**

Reiki is an energy healing approach that uses universal healing energy to bring balance to people mentally, emotionally, physically, and spiritually. **Reiki.org**

Somatic Experiencing (SE) is a trauma resolution approach developed by Peter Levine, PhD. It is a body-centered approach that uses the knowledge and tools from many disciplines, including neuroscience, physiology, and Indigenous healing practices, to help the client release shock and move through incomplete fight-or-flight reactions. **Traumahealing.org**

If you are feeling suicidal, please reach out for help.
U.S. National Suicide Hotline Number: 1-800-273-8255

References

Chapter 2

Bailey, B. (2010). Partner violence during pregnancy: Prevalence, effects, screening, and management. *International Journal of Women's Health*, 183.

Brand, S. R. (2006). The effect of maternal PTSD following in utero trauma exposure on behavior and temperament in the 9-month-old infant. *Annals of the New York Academy of Sciences*, *1071*(1), 454–458.

Dias, B. G., & Ressler, K. J. (2013). Parental olfactory experience influences behavior and neural structure in subsequent generations. *Nature Neuroscience*, *17*(1), 89–96.

Hurley, D. (2015, June 24). Grandma's experiences leave a mark in your genes. *Discover*. https://www.discovermagazine.com/health/grandmas-experiences-leave-a-mark-on-your-genes

Yehuda, R., & Lehrner, A. (2018). Intergenerational transmission of trauma effects: Putative role of epigenetic mechanisms. *World Psychiatry*, *17*(3), 243–257.

Chapter 3

Golomb, E. (1995). *Trapped in the mirror: Adult children of narcissists in their struggle for self.* W. Morrow.

Lawson, C. A. (2004). *Understanding the borderline mother: Helping her children transcend the intensely unpredictable and volatile relationship.* Rowan and Littlefield.

Chapter 4

Hendrix, H., & Hunt, H. (2020). *Getting the love you want: A guide for couples.* Simon & Schuster UK.

Chapter 5

Anderson, S. J. (Producer), Bernstein, J. (Writer), Bochner Spitz, M. (Writer), & Hall, D. (Writer). (2007). *Meet the Robinsons.* Walt Disney Pictures.

Chapter 6

Miller, C. (2020). *Know my name: A memoir.* Penguin Books.

Chapter 7

Walker, P. (2013). *Complex PTSD: From surviving to thriving.* CreateSpace.

Chapter 13

Maté, G. (2019). *When the body says no: The cost of hidden stress.* Vermilion.

van der Kolk, B. A. (2015). *The body keeps the score: Brain, mind, and body in the healing of trauma.* Penguin Books.

Pillar 1

Frankl, V. E. (2006). *Man's Search for Meaning.* Beacon Press.

Schwartz, R. (2013). *Your soul's gift: The healing power of the life you planned before you were born.* Watkins.

Pillar 2

Brown, B. (2020). *Gifts of imperfection.* Random House.

Burger, N. (Director), Daugherty, E. (Writer), Taylor, V. (Writer), & Roth, V. (Writer). (2014). *Divergent.* Summit Entertainment, Red Wagon Entertainment.

Levine, P. A. (2010). *In an unspoken voice: How the body releases trauma and restores goodness.* North Atlantic Books.

Pillar 3

Hicks, E., & Hicks, J. (2017). *Ask and it is given: Learning to manifest your desires.* Hay House (India).

Pillar 5

Tolle, E. (2020, October 19). *Eckhart on the dark night of the soul.* https://eckharttolle.com/eckhart-on-the-dark-night-of-the-soul/

Zukav, G. (1990). *The seat of the soul.* Free Press.

Pillar 6

Singer, M. A. (2015). *The surrender experiment: My journey into life's perfection.* Harmony Books.

Pillar 7

Walsch, N. D. (2016). *Conversations with God: An uncommon dialogue.* TarcherPerigee.

Pillar 9

Karpman, S. B. (2014). *A game free life: The definitive book on the drama triangle.* Drama Triangle Productions.

Pillar 10

Erivo, C. (2021). Georgia's School of Dance and Theatre. *Stand up.* [Video]. YouTube. https://www.youtube.com/watch?v=DxKfVyCGh24

Pillar 12

Dispenza, J. (2012). *Breaking the habit of being yourself: How to lose your mind and create a new one.* Hay House.

Pillar 13

Dispenza, J. (2017). *Becoming supernatural: How common people are doing the uncommon.* Hay House.

Pillar 15

Lammers, W. (2019). *Minute miracles: The practice of Logosynthesis.* Bristol House.

Pillar 16

Phelps-Roper, M. (2019). *Unfollow: A memoir of loving and leaving the Westboro Baptist Church.* Farrar, Straus, and Giroux.

Purdy, A. (2015). *On my own two feet: From losing my legs to learning the dance of life.* William Morrow.

Wagamese, R. (2012). *Indian horse.* Douglas & McIntyre.

Conclusion

Cohen, L. (1992). Anthem. On *The future.* Columbia Records.

Acknowledgments

The Persian mystical poet Rumi stated, "As you start to walk on the way, the way appears." For me, the way appeared, in part, through the many wonderful people who helped me along my path. I'm eternally grateful for the mentors, coaches, healers, and other support people who arrived, right on time, throughout my extensive journey.

To the one who has been with me the longest, my beloved husband Kyle, thank you. There have been no witnesses who can fully grasp the vast challenges that we have faced together. Your front row seat to the unfolding of my story has taken immense courage of your own and I am grateful for you.

To my children, Grace and Molly, the journey for the children of cycle breakers is not an easy one. You are strong women with so much compassion, wisdom, humor, and tenacity. It is a beautiful thing when your adult children are your friends. I'm a lucky lady to be your mother.

To Jim Kreider, the depth of compassion you can hold for someone in pain is extraordinary. For over four years you gently guided me through the initial stages of my trauma recovery and gave me hope, comfort, and a new template for safety in the presence of men.

To Monika Godos, thank you for guiding me through some of the most turbulent parts of my trauma recovery. Thank you for teaching me how to take full responsibility for my life. Your generous feedback on my book has been invaluable and you have lots of good karma on the way for all you have done for me.

To Amy Roden, thank you for showing up in my life as a healer when I truly felt I had hit my limits. You are my wise guide and my big sister (even though you are younger than me). Thank you for helping me to truly appreciate the power of amusement and blowing roses.

Space does not allow for me to give the detail I would like to personally thank everyone who has been my ally. With deep appreciation for you: Alba Valez, Dr. Alicia Johnson, Allie Horner, Amanda East, Amy Roden, Angie Schoenherr, Ann Varney, Anni Reynolds, Caroline Sharp, Carrie Bush, Cathy King, Christina Malicke, Cole Cottin, Damian Nola, Duane Kessler, Elaine Brewer, Erika Brose, Francesca Toman, Jim Kreider, Julie Ray, Karen Clarke, Karen Kessler, Kate Willingham, Laura Shaughnessy, Maggie Jones Boyle, Mary Leckie, Michelle Webb, Monika Godos, Pat McLaurin, Shawna Ristic, Shelley Sutton, Susan Privoznik, Suzie Sullivan, and Dr. Willem Lammers.

Thank you to those who read the draft of my book and offered valuable insights: Amy Roden, Anni Reynolds, Caroline Sharp, Cynthia Burgett, Damian Nola, Jina Kugler, Mary Leckie, Monika Godos, and Shelly Sutton.

Thank you to my editor Robyn Fritz, for challenging me to write the best version of this book that I could. Thank you to Carolyn Levin for the legal vetting of my book, Laurel Robinson for your proofreading, Monica Wells for the cover design and Bob Lanphear for your layout and production. Thank you all for the respect you had for both me and my book.

Thank you to all my clients for trusting me with your stories. It is a privilege to work with all of you.

We all play a role in one another's lives. Unknowingly and unintentionally, we may tell someone just what they need to hear at the right time. Our funny TikTok video may lift someone's spirits when they are feeling down. The smile, compliment, or any other interaction that seems innocuous may dramatically help to alter the course of someone's life. Thank you to all the random people along the way who provided the subtle nudges of encouragement and upliftment I needed. There were a lot of you.

Thank you to those who read my book. May your journey be made less heavy by the words on these pages.

About the Author

For her entire adult life, Mindi Kessler, PhD, has been a seeker in the quest to understand and resolve human suffering. Trained as a marriage and family therapist, with advanced degrees from Colorado State University and Kansas State University, she specializes in working with people with extensive histories of developmental trauma through her private psychotherapy practice and individual and group coaching and online courses.

After her own complex challenges of emotional suffering and chronic pain and illness, she had to put her career on hold to come to terms with the origins of her own anguish. Her personal journey into the depths of previously unaddressed wounding from childhood gave her the freedom from suffering that was necessary to transform her life. She truly knows what it means and what it takes to become a cycle breaker.

In this book, Dr. Kessler shares what it took for her to transcend her pain and create a vibrant and meaningful life as she discusses what others with developmental trauma can do to heal and live their own best lives.

Dr. Kessler has been married to her husband, Kyle, whom she adores, for nearly 25 years, and has two amazing young adult daughters, Grace and Molly.

www.ingramcontent.com/pod-product-compliance
Lightning Source LLC
Chambersburg PA
CBHW071151130626
46553CB00004B/1606

* 9 7 9 8 9 8 6 4 9 3 3 0 5 *